Essential
German Grammar

By

GUY STERN

Chairman,
Department of Germanic Languages and Literatures
University of Cincinnati

and

EVERETT F. BLEILER

DOVER PUBLICATIONS, INC.
NEW YORK

Essential German Grammar is a new work, first published by Dover Publications, Inc. in 1961.

International Standard Book Number: 0-486-20422-7
Library of Congress Catalog Card Number: 74-28533

Manufactured in the United States of America
Dover Publications, Inc.
31 East 2nd Street, Mineola, N.Y. 11501

Table of Contents

Introduction

Essential German Grammar assumes that you will be spending a limited number of hours studying German grammar and that your objective is simple everyday communication. It is offered not as a condensed outline of all aspects of the grammar, but as a series of aids which will enable you to use more effectively and with greater versatility phrases and vocabulary that you have previously learned. You will become familiar with the more common structures and patterns of the language and learn a selected number of the most useful rules and forms.

How to Study Essential German Grammar

If you have studied German in a conventional manner, you will probably understand everything in *Essential German Grammar*, which can then serve as a refresher even though it uses a different approach than conventional grammars. You may want to glance through the book and then pay attention to those areas in which you are weak.

But if this is the first time you have studied German grammar, the following suggestions will be helpful.

1. Don't approach this book until you have mastered several hundred useful phrases and expressions such as you will find in any good phrase book or the *Listen & Learn* course. Everything will be more comprehensible and usable after you have achieved some simple, working knowledge of the language. The purpose of this book is to enable you to achieve greater fluency with the phrase approach, not to teach you to construct sentences from rules and vocabulary.

2. Read *Essential German Grammar* through at least once in its entirety. Don't be concerned if sections are not immediately clear to you; on second or third reading, they will make better sense. This first reading is necessary to give you a better understanding

7

of certain terms and concepts used at the beginning. What may appear discouragingly difficult at first will become more understandable as your studies progress. As you use the language and hear it spoken, many aspects of German grammar will begin to form recognizable patterns. *Essential German Grammar* will acquaint you with the structure and some of the peculiarities of this grammar, and will be helpful to you in developing your vocabulary and in generally improving your comprehension.

3. Go back to this book periodically. Sections which seem difficult or of doubtful benefit to you now may prove extremely helpful later.

4. For the most part, *Essential German Grammar* is presented in a logical order, especially for the major divisions of grammar, and you will do best to follow its sequence in your studies. However, the authors are aware that some students learn best when they study to answer their immediate questions and needs (e.g., how to form the comparative; the declension of the verb *to be*, etc.). If you prefer to work in this manner, study entire sections and not only individual remarks.

5. Examples are given for every rule. You may find it helpful to memorize the examples. If you learn every example in this supplement and its literal translation, you will have been exposed to the most basic problems of German grammar and to models for their solution.

6. One cannot study German systematically without an understanding of its grammar, and the use and understanding of grammatical terms is as essential as a knowledge of certain mechanical terms when you learn to drive a car. If your knowledge of grammatical terms is weak, read the Glossary (p. 104) and refer to it whenever necessary.

There are many ways to express the same thought. Every language has several different constructions to convey a single idea; some simple, others difficult. An involved verb conjugation may well be a more sophisticated way of expressing a thought and one which you may ultimately wish to master, but during your first experiments in communication you can achieve your aim by using a simple construction. Throughout this grammar you will find helpful hints on how to avoid difficult constructions.

As you begin to speak German, you will be your own best judge of the areas in which you need help in grammatical construction. If there is no one with whom to practice, speak mentally to yourself. In the course of a day see how many of the simple thoughts you've expressed in English can be stated in some manner in German. This kind of experimental self-testing will give direction to your study of grammar. Remember that you are studying this course in German not to pass an examination or receive a certificate, but to communicate with others on a simple but useful level. *Essential German Grammar* is not the equivalent of a formal course of study at a university. Although it could serve as a supplement to such a course, its primary aim is to help the adult study on his own. Indeed, no self-study or academic course or series could ever be offered that is ideally suited to every student. You must therefore rely on and be guided by your own rate of learning and your own requirements and interests.

If this grammar or any other grammar tends to inhibit your use of the language you may have learned through a simple phrase approach as taught in some schools and the *Listen and Learn* records, curtail your study of grammar until you really feel it will assist rather than hinder your speaking. Your objective is speaking, and you *can* learn to speak a language without formal grammatical training. The fundamental purpose of *Essential German Grammar* is to enable you to learn more rapidly and eliminate hit-or-miss memorization. For those who prefer a more systematic approach, grammar does enable them to learn more quickly.

At the risk of being repetitious, the author must again urge you not to be afraid of making mistakes. The purpose of this grammar is not to teach you to speak like a native but to communicate and make yourself understood. If its goal is achieved, you will be speaking German and making mistakes rather than maintaining a discreet silence. You will most certainly make errors in declensional endings which are difficult for the English-speaking student to master, but don't let fear of incorrect endings deter you from speaking. Sooner or later you'll review *Essential German Grammar* or a more detailed book at a time that is appropriate for polishing your speech.

Suggestions for Vocabulary Building

The following suggestions may be helpful to you in building your vocabulary:

1. Study words and word lists that answer real and preferably immediate personal needs. If you are planning to travel in the near future your motivation and orientation is clear cut and *Listen and Learn German* or a good travel phrase book will give you the material you need. Select material according to your personal interests and requirements. If you don't plan to motor, don't spend time studying parts of the car. If you like foreign foods, study the supplementary foreign food list in *Say It In German*. Even if you do not plan to travel in the near future, you will probably learn more quickly by imagining a travel or real life situation.

2. Use the association technique for memorization. For the most part, *Listen and Learn German* or travel phrase books give you associated word lists. If you continue to build your vocabulary by memorization, don't use a dictionary for this purpose. Select such grammars or books that have lists of word families.

3. Study the specialized vocabulary of your profession, business, or hobby. If you are interested in real estate, learn the many terms associated with property, buying, selling, leasing, etc. An interest in mathematics should lead you to a wide vocabulary in this science. Words in your specialty will be learned quickly and a surprising amount will be applicable or transferable to other areas. Although these specialized vocabularies may not always be readily available, an active interest and a good dictionary will help you get started.

Abbreviations and Note

Abbreviations Used in *Essential German Grammar*

MASC.	Masculine
FEM.	Feminine
NEUT.	Neuter
SING.	Singular
PL.	Plural
LIT.	Literally
NOM.	Nominative
GEN.	Genitive
DAT.	Dative
ACC.	Accusative
INFIN.	Infinitive
PART.	Participle

Note: Whenever the German construction is basically different from the construction in English, a *literal* translation enclosed in brackets is given to help you analyze and understand the German syntax. This literal translation is immediately followed by a translation into idiomatic English.

How to Turn Statements into Questions

1. Any statement in German can be turned into a question by inverting the word order, that is, by letting the working verb precede the subject.

Wir kommen heute an.
We arrive today.

Kommen wir heute an?
[*Come we* today on?]
Do we arrive today?

Er hat Geld.
He has money.

Hat er Geld?
[*Has he* money?]
Does he have money?

Er kann uns die Stadt zeigen.
[*He can* us the city show.]
He can show us the city.

Kann er uns die Stadt zeigen?
[*Can he* us the city show?]
Can he show us the city?

2. The following interrogative words are of great help in formulating questions. Memorize them. Note that when you use an interrogative, the inverted word order is still used.

wann	when	wer	who
wo	where	was	what
wie	how	was für	what kind of
wieviel	how much		

Wann kommt er?
[*When comes* he?]
When will he come?

Wo ist das Hotel?
Where is the hotel?

Wie komme ich zur Kirche?
[*How come* I to the church?]
How do I get to the church?

Wieviel kostet das?
[*How much costs* this?]
How much does this cost?

Wer hat angerufen?
[*Who has* called?]
Who called?

Was soll ich machen?
What should I do?

Was für ein Hotel *ist* es?
What kind of a hotel *is* it?

How to Negate Statements

In English we can turn ordinary affirmative statements into negative statements by inserting the words *not* or *no*: I can come, I can *not* come; I will have time tomorrow, I will have *no* time tomorrow. In German much the same procedure is followed with the key words *nicht* and *kein*. For the declension and use of *kein* see pp. 28–31.

As soon as you introduce *nicht* into a sentence, your listener will understand that you are communicating a negative idea. The only problem with *nicht* is its position in the sentence, which is not the same as the English word "not." Although no rule can be given that will cover every instance, the following rules will help you most of the time.

1. If you have a simple verb in an independent clause, *nicht* follows the verb and its objects (if there are any):

Ich gehe *nicht.*   Ich verstehe das *nicht.*
[I go *not.*]   [I understand that *not.*]
I do*n't* go.   I do*n't* understand this.

Ich gehe heute *nicht* ins Kino.
[I go today *not* to the movies.]
I do*n't* go to the movies today.

2. When you have past participles, infinitives, or separable prefixes in the sentence, *nicht* is usually placed immediately before them.

Er hat uns die Geschichte *nicht erzählt.*
[He has us the story *not told.*]
He did*n't tell* us the story.

Wir werden uns das Museum *nicht ansehen.*
[We will ourselves the museum *not look-at.*]
We wo*n't visit* the museum.

14

Sie kamen gestern *nicht an.*
[They came yesterday *not on.*]
They did *not arrive* yesterday.

Ich kann *nicht mitkommen,* weil ich morgen *nicht abfahren* kann.
[I can *not come along,* because I tomorrow *not depart* can.]
I can*not come along,* because I can*not leave* tomorrow.

In the first sentence, *nicht* is placed immediately before the past participle *erzählt*; in the second sentence before the infinitive *ansehen*; in the third sentence before the separable prefix *an.* In the fourth sentence, *nicht* is placed before the infinitive *mitkommen,* and before the infinitive *abfahren.* Observe that the second clause is a dependent clause, with a working verb at the end; the word order in such a clause is not the same as in independent clauses with simple verbs. (See p. 85 for placement of past participles, infinitives, and separable prefixes.)

3. As in English, *nicht* precedes a particular word or phrase if *nicht* modifies this word or phrase, rather than the whole sentence.

Er kommt leider *nicht heute,* sondern morgen.
[He comes unfortunately *not today,* but tomorrow.]
Unfortunately, he is coming *not today,* but tomorrow.

Nouns

Using Nouns in German

In English sentences, you generally add endings on nouns in two situations: to form possessives and to form plurals. You add -'*s* to most nouns to indicate possession (ship'*s* bell, girl'*s* dress, etc.) and -*s* or -*es* to form the plural (bird*s*, watch*es*, hand*s*, etc.).

The same general principles hold in German, but the rules are more complex. There are more endings, and more occasions when endings are added. The mechanics of declension, however, are not as difficult as they are said to be, and with the aid of a few rules you can master them easily.

In German there are five important ways (or declensions) in which nouns take endings and you must know to which declension a noun belongs before you can use it properly. (In English almost all nouns take -*s* or -*es* to form their plural, but there are remnants of other declensions in such words as ox, oxen; man, men; sheep, sheep, which form their plurals in other ways.)

There are no watertight rules for knowing which nouns belong to which declension, but there are good general hints which will lead you to the proper ending most of the time. Before you study the five declensions, learn these rules,because it has been estimated that they cover more than 95% of the words you are likely to use, and with them, you will be able to handle most German nouns without looking at involved tables of declension.

Rule 1. Feminine nouns never take endings to form their singular cases. They use the same form for nominative, genitive, dative, and accusative.

	(the typewriter)	(the street)
NOM.	die Schreibmaschine	die Strasse
GEN.	der Schreibmaschine	der Strasse

16

DAT.	der Schreibmaschine	der Strasse
ACC.	die Schreibmaschine	die Strasse

Rule 2. All neuter nouns and almost all masculine nouns require only one ending in the singular. This is *-s* or *-es*, which is added to the noun to form the genitive. (It is true that some masculine and neuter nouns that are only one syllable long can add *-e* to form the dative singular, but this ending is optional and can be ignored.)

	(the shoe) MASC.	(the shirt) NEUT.
NOM.	der Schuh	das Hemd
GEN.	des Schuh*es*	des Hemd*es*
DAT.	dem Schuh	dem Hemd
ACC.	den Schuh	das Hemd

Rule 3. Masculine nouns designating living beings usually add *-n* to form all other cases, both singular and plural, if the nominative singular ends in *-e*.

	SING. (the lion[s])	PL.
NOM.	der Löw*e*	die Löw*en*
GEN.	des Löw*en*	der Löw*en*
DAT.	dem Löw*en*	den Löw*en*
ACC.	den Löw*en*	die Löw*en*

Rule 4. All dative plural forms end in *-n* or *-en*.

	MASC. (the man)	FEM. (the woman)	NEUT. (the child)
NOM. SING.	der Mann	die Frau	das Kind
DAT. PL.	den Männer*n*	den Frau*en*	den Kinder*n*

	(the spoon)	(the knife)
NOM. SING.	der Löffel	das Messer
DAT. PL.	den Löffel*n*	den Messer*n*

Rule 5. In the respective plurals of all declensions and all genders, the nominative, genitive, and accusative always have identical forms.

	MASC. (the forest)	FEM. (the pear)	NEUT. (the cloth)
NOM. SING.	der Wald	die Birne	das Tuch
NOM. PL.	die Wälder	die Birnen	die Tücher
GEN. PL.	der Wälder	der Birnen	der Tücher
ACC. PL.	die Wälder	die Birnen	die Tücher

To form the dative plural of the above nouns, add -*(e)n* to the nominative plural of the noun, unless the nominative plural already ends in -*(e)n*. If the nominative plural ends in -*(e)n*, then the dative plural will be identical with the nominative, genitive, and accusative plural forms. Thus the dative plural of the above nouns is, respectively, *den Wäldern, den Birnen, den Tüchern.*

Noun Groups

Every German noun belongs to one of five declensions, and its endings change according to the declension to which it belongs. Although most singular forms can be determined by the first three rules in the preceding section, plural forms are more complex. While there are no simple or exhaustive rules for determining what plural form a noun will take, there are some general rules which may make memorization of forms easier for you.

Group I. The characteristic of this declension is that it takes no endings for its plural forms, except for the necessary -*n* in the dative (see rule 4, p. 17). An umlaut is often added to the stem vowel to make the plural forms.* Singular forms follow the rules given in the preceding section.

SINGULAR

	(the father)	(the mother)	(the building)
NOM.	der Vater	die Mutter	das Gebäude
GEN.	des Vaters	der Mutter	des Gebäudes
DAT.	dem Vater	der Mutter	dem Gebäude
ACC.	den Vater	die Mutter	das Gebäude

* See p. 93 for a discussion of the umlaut.

PLURAL

NOM.	die Väter	die Mütter	die Gebäude
GEN.	der Väter	der Mütter	der Gebäude
DAT.	den Vätern	den Müttern	den Gebäuden
ACC.	die Väter	die Mütter	die Gebäude

Some nouns that belong to Group I: most nouns whose nominative singular ends in *-el*, *-en*, or *-er*; neuter nouns that begin with *Ge-* and end in *-e*.

Group II. The nouns that belong to this declension add *-e* (*-en* in the dative) to form their plurals. They sometimes umlaut their stem vowel in the plural. Singular forms follow the three rules given on pp. 16–17.

SINGULAR

	(the arm)	(the fruit)	(the piece)
NOM.	der Arm	die Frucht	das Stück
GEN.	des Armes	der Frucht	des Stückes
DAT.	dem Arm	der Frucht	dem Stück
ACC.	den Arm	die Frucht	das Stück

PLURAL

NOM.	die Arme	die Früchte	die Stücke
GEN.	der Arme	der Früchte	der Stücke
DAT.	den Armen	den Früchten	den Stücken
ACC.	die Arme	die Früchte	die Stücke

Nouns that belong to Group II: most masculine nouns that are one syllable long; about half the feminine and neuter nouns that are one syllable long.

Group III. Nouns in this group add *-er* (*-ern* in the dative) to form their plurals, and place an umlaut over the vowel wherever possible. Singular forms follow the three rules given on pp. 16–17.

SINGULAR

	(the man)	(the glass)
NOM.	der Mann	das Glas
GEN.	des Mannes	des Glases
DAT.	dem Mann	dem Glas
ACC.	den Mann	das Glas

PLURAL

NOM.	die Männer	die Gläser
GEN.	der Männer	der Gläser
DAT.	den Männern	den Gläsern
ACC.	die Männer	die Gläser

Nouns that belong to Group III: many neuter nouns that are only one syllable long. There are no feminine nouns in this group.

Group IV. This is sometimes called the weak declension of nouns. Nouns in this group add -n or -en to form all plurals,—nominative, genitive, dative, and accusative. The feminine singular forms take no ending, as explained in Rule 1 on p. 16. Masculine singular nouns add -en to form all cases except the nominative, and often fit Rule 3, p. 17. None of the nouns in this group ever umlaut the stem vowel in the plural.

SINGULAR

	(the student)	(the woman, wife)	(the bridge)
NOM.	der Student	die Frau	die Brücke
GEN.	des Studenten	der Frau	der Brücke
DAT.	dem Studenten	der Frau	der Brücke
ACC.	den Studenten	die Frau	die Brücke

PLURAL

NOM.	die Studenten	die Frauen	die Brücken
GEN.	der Studenten	der Frauen	der Brücken
DAT.	den Studenten	den Frauen	den Brücken
ACC.	die Studenten	die Frauen	die Brücken

Nouns that belong to Group IV: most feminine nouns that are more than one syllable long; most masculine nouns denoting living things. There are no neuter nouns in this group.

Group V. This small group includes nouns of foreign origin. They are declined similarly to English nouns, with *-s* for the genitive singular, and *-s* for the plural.

	SING.	(the auto)	PL.
NOM.	das Auto		die Auto*s*
GEN.	des Auto*s*		der Auto*s*
DAT.	dem Auto		den Auto*s*
ACC.	das Auto		die Auto*s*

Other common words in this group are *das Radio, das Hotel,* and *das Restaurant.*

Irregular Nouns

There are a few nouns whose declension in the genitive singular is irregular. The irregularity consists of their adding *-ns* or *-ens* to form the genitive singular, instead of adding only *-s* or *-es,* according to Rule 2, p. 17. The plurals of these nouns are formed by adding *-n* or *-en* to the stem of the noun, and all the plural forms are identical. It may help you to think of these nouns as belonging to Group IV, as far as their plural forms are concerned. The three most common nouns of this type are given below:

SINGULAR

	(the heart)	(the peace)	(the name)
NOM.	das Herz	der Friede	der Name
GEN.	des Herz*ens*	des Fried*ens*	des Nam*ens*
DAT.	dem Herzen	dem Frieden	dem Namen
ACC.	das Herz*	den Frieden	den Namen

* Note: ACC. is identical to NOM.

PLURAL

NOM.	die Herz*en*	(Friede has	die Nam*en*
GEN.	der Herz*en*	no plural.)	der Nam*en*
DAT.	den Herz*en*		den Nam*en*
ACC.	die Herz*en*		die Nam*en*

As you can see, the plural of these two nouns is regular, that is, they use the form of the nominative plural throughout.

Mixed Declensions

A few nouns use the typical -*s* or -*es* for the genitive singular ending, in accordance with Rule 2, but form their plurals as if they belonged to Group IV, that is by adding -*n* or -*en* to the noun stem and using the same form throughout the plural. *Das Bett* is a typical mixed-declension noun to use as a model.

SINGULAR

	(the bed)	(the eye)	(the lake)
NOM.	das Bett	das Auge	der See
GEN.	des Bett*es*	des Auge*s*	des See*s*
DAT.	dem Bett	dem Auge	dem See
ACC.	das Bett	das Auge	den See

PLURAL

NOM.	die Bett*en*	die Auge*n*	die See*n*
GEN.	der Bett*en*	der Auge*n*	der See*n*
DAT.	den Bett*en*	den Auge*n*	den See*n*
ACC.	die Bett*en*	die Auge*n*	die See*n*

Articles and Pronominal Adjectives

Gender and the Definite Article

German nouns each belong to one of three genders: masculine, feminine, or neuter. This is purely a grammatical classification, and need not be related to the sex of the person or thing concerned. Inanimate or sexless objects and abstract ideas are classified as masculine, feminine, or neuter solely because of the pattern of the language.

MASC.		FEM.	
der Löffel	(the spoon)	*die* Gabel	(the fork)
der Mann	(the man)	*die* Frau	(the woman)
der Kredit	(the credit)	*die* Freiheit	(the freedom)
der Zug	(the train)	*die* Kartoffel	(the potato)

NEUT.	
das Mädchen	(the girl)
das Meer	(the sea)
das Fenster	(the window)
das Fräulein	(the young lady)

There are no easy rules for determining the gender of a noun. However, in most instances, male persons will be masculine, and female persons will be feminine; but this is not always the case, as you can see from *das Mädchen* (neuter) above. All nouns that end in *-chen* or *-lein,* as for example, *Mädchen* and *Fräulein,* above, are neuter.

Do not try to learn many very complex rules for determining the gender of nouns. Instead, memorize the definite article with each noun.

The Word for "the"
(The Definite Article)

In English we have only a single form to express the definite article in all grammatical situations. We always say *the*. In German the definite article is more complex and changes according to the case, number, and gender of the noun it accompanies. The German definite article always "agrees" with the accompanying noun; that is, it takes the same case, gender, and number as that noun.* The forms of the German definite article are given below:

SINGULAR

	MASC.	FEM.	NEUT.
NOM.	der	die	das
GEN.	des	der	des
DAT.	dem	der	dem
ACC.	den	die	das

PLURAL
(all genders)

NOM.	die
GEN.	der
DAT.	den
ACC.	die

Memorize these forms, for they are very important. *Der-die-das* is one of the most common words in German, and the endings it displays are also used to form independent adjectives and certain pronominal adjectives (see p. 27 and 35).

Observe that there are patterns in the declension of *der-die-das*:

1. The nominative and accusative forms of the feminine article are identical, as are the respective forms of the neuter article.

2. In the genitive and dative cases singular, the masculine and neuter forms are identical.

---

* See p. 113 if you are not clear about the concept of case.

3. Feminine singular forms are the same in the genitive and dative.

4. All genders share the same forms in the plural.

5. *Der* functions for a masculine noun in the nominative case, but is also used for a feminine noun in the genitive and dative cases, and for the genitive plural of all nouns.

The Words for "a" and "an"
(The Indefinite Article)

The German words *ein-eine-ein*, which correspond to "a" and "an" in English, agree in case and gender with the noun they accompany.   Their forms are:

	MASC.	FEM.	NEUT.
NOM.	ein	eine	ein
GEN.	eines	einer	eines
DAT.	einem	einer	einem
ACC.	einen	eine	ein

Observe that the declension of the masculine and neuter indefinite articles is identical, except for the accusative forms.

Naturally there are no plural forms for *ein-eine-ein*, just as there are none in English for "a" or "an."*

Können Sie mir *einen* Arzt empfehlen?
[Can you to me a doctor recommend?]
Can you recommend a doctor to me?

The noun, *(der) Arzt*, in the above sentence, is masculine, and appears here in the accusative case because it is the direct object of the verb, *empfehlen*.   It is therefore necessary to express the indefinite article in the masculine accusative form, *einen*.

---

* The German definite article, *der-die-das*, and the indefinite article, *ein-eine-ein*, are generally used in the same situations as their counterparts in English.

Examples of the Definite Article

(Showing Agreement with Noun in Case, Gender, and Number)

SINGULAR

	MASC. NOUN	FEM. NOUN	NEUT. NOUN
NOM.	*Der* Reiseführer kommt. The guide comes.	*Die* Strassenbahn kommt. The streetcar comes.	*Das* Schiff kommt. The ship comes.
GEN.	Die Antwort *des* Reiseführers. [The answer of the guide.] The guide's answer.	Die Nummer *der* Strassenbahn. [The number of the streetcar.] The streetcar's number.	Die Farbe *des* Schiffes. [The color of the ship.] The ship's color.
DAT.	Wir gehen mit *dem* Reiseführer. We go with the guide.	Wir fahren mit *der* Strassenbahn. We travel with the streetcar.	Wir fahren mit *dem* Schiff. We travel with the ship.
ACC.	Wir sehen *den* Reiseführer. We see the guide.	Wir sehen *die* Strassenbahn. We see the streetcar.	Wir sehen *das* Schiff. We see the ship.

PLURAL

	MASC. NOUN	FEM. NOUN	NEUT. NOUN
NOM.	Die Reiseführer kommen. The guides come.	Die Strassenbahnen kommen. The streetcars come.	Die Schiffe kommen. The ships come.
GEN.	Die Antwort *der* Reiseführer. [The answer of the guides.] The guides' answer.	Die Nummer *der* Strassenbahnen. [The number of the streetcars.] The streetcars' number.	Die Farbe *der* Schiffe. [The color of the ships.] The ships' color.
DAT.	Wir gehen mit *den* Reiseführern. We go with the guides.	Wir fahren mit *den* Strassenbahnen. We travel with the streetcars.	Wir fahren mit *den* Schiffen. We travel with the ships.
ACC.	Wir sehen *die* Reiseführer. We see the guides.	Wir sehen *die* Strassenbahnen. We see the streetcars.	Wir sehen *die* Schiffe. We see the ships.

The "*der*-words"

Certain pronominal adjectives take the same endings, when they are declined, as the definite article, *der-die-das*.* Because of this similarity in declension, these words are called "*der*-words." The most common are:

dieser	this
jener	that
jeder	every
welcher	which

We shall decline only one of these words in full; the others are all declined in the same manner.

SINGULAR

	MASC.	FEM.	NEUT.
NOM.	dies*er*	dies*e*	dies*es*
GEN.	dies*es*	dies*er*	dies*es*
DAT.	dies*em*	dies*er*	dies*em*
ACC.	dies*en*	dies*e*	dies*es*

PLURAL
(all genders)

NOM.	dies*e*
GEN.	dies*er*
DAT.	dies*en*
ACC.	dies*e*

Wieviel kostet dies*es* Zimmer?
[How much costs this room?]
How much does this room cost?

The pronominal adjective, *dieses*, in the above sentence, is nominative, neuter, singular, because the noun, *Zimmer*, to which it refers, is neuter and appears in the nominative case as the subject of the sentence.

---

* See p. 28 for pronominal adjectives which are declined differently.

Von *welchem* Bahnsteig fährt *dieser* Zug ab?
[From which platform travels this train off?]
From which platform does this train leave?

The word *welchem* is dative, masculine, singular because it must agree with *Bahnsteig*, a masculine noun which takes the dative case as the object of the preposition *von*. *Dieser* is nominative, singular, masculine since *Zug*, which it modifies, is a masculine noun here used in the nominative case as the subject of the sentence.

The "*ein*-words"

A group of pronominal adjectives are declined just like *ein-eine-ein*, and, like the indefinite article, agree in case, gender, and number with the noun they modify. The most common "*ein*-words" are:

mein	my	unser	our
sein	his, its	ihr	their
ihr	her	Ihr	your (polite)
kein	no, not any		

We shall decline only one of these words in full, as the others are all declined in the same manner.

SINGULAR

	MASC.	FEM.	NEUT.
NOM.	mein	mein*e*	mein
GEN.	mein*es*	mein*er*	mein*es*
DAT.	mein*em*	mein*er*	mein*em*
ACC.	mein*en*	mein*e*	mein

PLURAL
(all genders)

NOM.	mein*e*
GEN.	mein*er*
DAT.	mein*en*
ACC.	mein*e*

Examples of "*ein-words*"

(Showing Agreement with Noun in Case, Gender, and Number)

SINGULAR

	MASC. NOUN	FEM. NOUN	NEUT. NOUN
NOM.	*Mein* Garten ist schön. My garden is nice.	*Meine* Blume ist schön. My flower is nice.	*Mein* Zimmer ist schön. My room is nice.
GEN.	Die Blumen *meines* Gartens. The flowers of my garden.	Die Farbe *meiner* Blume. The color of my flower.	Die Grösse *meines* Zimmers. The size of my room.
DAT.	Ich sitze in *meinem* Garten. I sit in my garden.	Ich spreche von *meiner* Blume. I speak about my flower.	Ich bleibe in *meinem* Zimmer. I remain in my room.
ACC.	Ich sehe *meinen* Garten. I see my garden.	Ich sehe *meine* Blume. I see my flower.	Ich vermiete *mein* Zimmer. I sublet my room.

PLURAL

	MASC. NOUN	FEM. NOUN	NEUT. NOUN
NOM.	*Meine* Gärten sind schön. My gardens are nice.	*Meine* Blumen sind schön. My flowers are nice.	*Meine* Zimmer sind schön. My rooms are nice.
GEN.	Die Blumen *meiner* Gärten. The flowers of my gardens.	Die Farben *meiner* Blumen. The colors of my flowers.	Die Fenster *meiner* Zimmer. The windows of my room.
DAT.	Ich spreche von *meinen* Gärten. I speak about my gardens.	Ich spreche von *meinen* Blumen. I speak about my flowers.	Ich spreche von *meinen* Zimmern. I speak about my rooms.
ACC.	Ich sehe *meine* Gärten. I see my gardens.	Ich sehe *meine* Blumen. I see my flowers.	Ich sehe *meine* Zimmer. I see my rooms.

Study this declension and the examples that follow; then refer back to the declension of the *"der*-words." You will note many similarities. Only the singular forms differ from the *der* forms, and even here the differences are minor, although important for meaning. The endings for all plurals are, in fact, identical for the *"der*-words" and *"ein*-words."

The Word "kein"

The word *kein* deserves special comment, since its use is often difficult for the student. *Kein* is a negative adjective, and corresponds to the English word *no*, when *no* is used to modify a noun.

Wir werden *keine* Zeit für Museen haben.
[We shall *no* time for museums have.]
We shall have *no* time for museums.

Ich habe *keine* Briefe für Sie.
I have *no* letters for you.

In English we have two ways of making a sentence negative. We can use the idea of negation with nouns, as in the English sentences above, or we can express the same idea by associating the idea of negation with the verb, and using the adverb *not*: We shall *not* have time for museums. I do *not* have any letters for you. Both ways are grammatically correct, but we usually prefer the idea of verbal negation: We shall *not* have time, instead of we shall have *no* time.

The German adverb *nicht* corresponds to the English adverb *not*, and the adjective *kein* to the English modifier *no*. In use, however, German differs from English. When speaking German, you should use the *kein* form whenever possible because it is preferred usage. It is as if you transferred every English negative sentence to a "no" form. Thus, you should *not* say in literal translation:

Ich möchte heute *nicht* ein Frühstück.
[I want today *not* a breakfast.]

But you should say:

Ich möchte heute *kein* Frühstück.
[I want today *no* breakfast.]
I don't want any breakfast today.

Or, instead of saying:

Wir haben noch *nicht* Billets gekauft.
[We have yet *not* tickets bought.]
We have not yet bought tickets.

Say:

Wir haben noch *keine* Billets gekauft.
[We have yet *no* tickets bought.]
We haven't bought any tickets yet.

Adjectives and Adverbs

Adjective Endings

In English, adjectives are undeclined; our adjectives keep the same form in all situations, and do not take endings to show agreement in case, gender, and number with the noun they accompany. German adjectives are more complex because they can take many endings that differ according to the words they accompany. There are three separate series of endings for adjectives:

1. Endings used when an adjective is preceded by the definite article (*der-die-das*) or a "*der*-word."

2. Endings used when an adjective is preceded by the indefinite article (*ein-eine-ein*) or an "*ein*-word."

3. Endings used when an adjective is independent.

Adjectives with "*der*-words"

Refer to p. 24 where the declension of *der-die-das* is discussed, and to p. 27 where the declension of *dieser* (this), *jener* (that), *jeder* (every), and *welcher* (which) is discussed. You will recall that these four words are called "*der*-words" because they take the same endings as the German word for *the*.

When adjectives are preceded by the definite article (*der-die-das*) or by a "*der*-word," they are declined as follows:

SINGULAR

	MASC. NOUN	FEM. NOUN
	(the English garden)	(the English city)
NOM.	der englische Garten.	die englische Stadt.
GEN.	des englischen Gartens.	der englischen Stadt.
DAT.	dem englischen Garten.	der englischen Stadt.
ACC.	den englischen Garten.	die englische Stadt.

NEUT. NOUN (SING.)

(the English book)

NOM.	das englische Buch.
GEN.	des englischen Buches.
DAT.	dem englischen Buch.
ACC.	das englische Buch.

PLURAL

	MASC. NOUN	FEM. NOUN
	(the English gardens)	(the English cities)
NOM.	die englischen Gärten.	die englischen Städte.
GEN.	der englischen Gärten.	der englischen Städte.
DAT.	den englischen Gärten.	den englischen Städten.
ACC.	die englischen Gärten.	die englischen Städte.

NEUT. NOUN

(the English books)

NOM.	die englischen Bücher.
GEN.	der englischen Bücher.
DAT.	den englischen Büchern.
ACC.	die englischen Bücher.

As you will observe, the only forms which do not take -*en* as an ending are the three nominative singular forms and the feminine and neuter accusative singular forms.   This set of endings is then simple to memorize: the ending is -*en* throughout, except in the nominative singular and the feminine and neuter accusative singular where it is -*e*.

Ich würde gern den deutschen Film sehen.
[I would gladly the German film see.]
I would like to see the German film.

Wo ist der nächste Flugplatz?
Where is the nearest airfield?

Diese süsse Marmelade schmeckt mir nicht.
[This sweet marmalade pleases me not.]
I don't like this sweet marmalade.

Adjectives with "*ein*-words"

Refer to p. 25 where the forms are given for the declension of *ein-eine-ein* (a, an), and to p. 28 where the declension of *mein* (my), *sein* (his, its), *ihr* (her), *kein* (no, not any), *unser* (our), *ihr* (their), and *Ihr* (your) is discussed. You will recall that these words are called "*ein*-words" because they take the same endings in the singular as *ein*.

Adjectives that are preceded by the indefinite article or any form of any of the "*ein*-words" take the following endings:

SINGULAR

	MASC.	FEM.
	(a good cheese)	(a good trip)
NOM.	ein gut*er* Käse	eine gut*e* Reise.
GEN.	eines gut*en* Käses.	einer gut*en* Reise.
DAT.	einem gut*en* Käse.	einer gut*en* Reise.
ACC.	einen gut*en* Käse.	eine gut*e* Reise.

	NEUT.
	(a good book)
NOM.	ein gut*es* Buch.
GEN.	eines gut*en* Buches.
DAT.	einem gut*en* Buch.
ACC.	ein gut*es* Buch.

PLURAL

	MASC.	FEM.
	(my good cheeses)	(my good trips)
NOM.	meine gut*en* Käse.	meine gut*en* Reisen.
GEN.	meiner gut*en* Käse.	meiner gut*en* Reisen.
DAT.	meinen gut*en* Käsen.	meinen gut*en* Reisen.
ACC.	meine gut*en* Käse.	meine gut*en* Reisen.

	NEUT.
	(my good books)
NOM.	meine gut*en* Bücher.
GEN.	meiner gut*en* Bücher.
DAT.	meinen gut*en* Büchern.
ACC.	meine gut*en* Bücher.

As you will notice, the only adjective forms that do not take -en are the same ones that do not take -en when the adjective is preceded by a "*der*-word" (pp. 32–33): all forms of the nominative singular, and the feminine and neuter accusative singular. As a further memory aid, note that the feminine nominative and accusative forms are identical, and that the neuter nominative and accusative forms are also alike.

Hier ist meine neu*e* Fahrkarte.
Here is my new ticket (for a train).

Das ist ein offen*er* Wagen.
That is an open car.

Können Sie ein englisch*es* Rezept füllen?
[Can you an English prescription fill?]
Can you fill an English prescription?

Ich will kein billig*es* Opernglas kaufen.
[I want no cheap opera glass to buy.]
I do not want to buy a cheap opera glass.

In the first example, *neue* is feminine, nominative, singular because *die Fahrkarte*, a feminine noun, is used in the nominative case as a predicate noun.

In the second example, *offener* is masculine, nominative, singular because *der Wagen*, a masculine noun, is also the predicate noun.

Englisches in the third sentence, and *billiges* in the fourth, both end in -*es* because they are neuter, accusative, singular. *Das Rezept* and *das Opernglas* are both used as direct objects which require the accusative case.

Independent Adjectives

An adjective which is not preceded by any of the "*der*-words" or "*ein*-words," or by either the definite or indefinite article, takes the following endings:

SINGULAR

	MASC. NOUN	FEM. NOUN	NEUT. NOUN
	(black coffee)	(warm milk)	(bad weather)
NOM.	schwarz*er* Kaffee	warm*e* Milch	schlecht*es* Wetter
GEN.	schwarz*en* Kaffees	warm*er* Milch	schlecht*en* Wetters
DAT.	schwarz*em* Kaffee	warm*er* Milch	schlecht*em* Wetter
ACC.	schwarz*en* Kaffee	warm*e* Milch	schlecht*es* Wetter

PLURAL
(all genders)
(green apples)

NOM.	grün*e* Äpfel
GEN.	grün*er* Äpfel
DAT.	grün*en* Äpfeln
ACC.	grün*e* Äpfel

These endings are known as strong endings. They are the same as those used on the "*der*-words" themselves, except in the masculine and neuter genitive singular where the ending is -*en* instead of -*s*.

Haben Sie frisch*es* Brot?
Do you have fresh bread?

Möbliert*e* Wohnungen sind nicht leicht zu finden.
Furnished apartments are not easy to find.

Das sind ausländisch*e* Poststempel.
Those are foreign postmarks.

Predicate Adjectives

When adjectives are used as predicate adjectives, that is, when they are used after a verb of being to express something about the subject of the sentence, they do not take endings, but are used in their basic form. Remember this rule of thumb: whenever the adjective follows the noun it modifies it is invariable, i.e., never declined.

Dieses Brot ist nicht *frisch*.
This bread is not fresh.

Ist dieses Haus *möbliert*?
Is this house furnished?

Dieser Käse bleibt lange *frisch*.
[This cheese stays long fresh.]
This cheese stays fresh for a long time.

Comparison of Adjectives

German adjectives form the comparative and superlative forms in much the same way as do English adjectives. In most instances, the comparative is formed by adding -er to the basic German adjective (or simply -r if the adjective already ends in -e), and the superlative is formed by adding -st or -est to the adjective. The -est ending is added to adjectives which end in d, t, s, or z, to make the ending fully audible. You never use the German equivalent of *more* or *most* as is often done in English.

POSITIVE		COMPARATIVE		SUPERLATIVE	
fein	fine	feiner	finer	feinst	finest
schön	nice	schöner	nicer	schönst	nicest
leise	soft, low	leiser	softer, lower	leisest	softest, lowest
heiss	hot	heisser	hotter	heissest	hottest
alt	old	älter	older	ältest	oldest
interessant		interessanter		interessantest	
interesting		more interesting		most interesting	

As you will observe, the adjective *alt* takes an umlaut in its comparative and superlative forms. Many other common one-syllable adjectives also umlaut if their stem vowel permits an umlaut. (See p. 93 for discussion of the umlaut.) Examples of such adjectives are:

POSITIVE		COMPARATIVE		SUPERLATIVE	
arm	poor	ärmer	poorer	ärmst	poorest
jung	young	jünger	younger	jüngst	youngest

POSITIVE		COMPARATIVE		SUPERLATIVE	
kalt	cold	kälter	colder	kältest	coldest
krank	sick	kränker	sicker	kränkst	sickest
kurz	short	kürzer	shorter	kürzest	shortest
lang	long	länger	longer	längst	longest
stark	strong	stärker	stronger	stärkst	strongest
warm	warm	wärmer	warmer	wärmst	warmest

Many other one-syllable adjectives, on the other hand, do not take an umlaut. There is no general rule. Either memorize the comparative form of the adjective or else consult your dictionary.

As in English, certain adjectives form their comparatives and superlatives irregularly:

POSITIVE		COMPARATIVE		SUPERLATIVE	
gut	good	besser	better	best	best
viel	much	mehr	more	meist	most
hoch	high	höher	higher	höchst	highest
nah	near	näher	nearer	nächst	nearest, next

Using the Comparative and Superlative of Adjectives

Comparatives and superlatives of adjectives are treated just like other adjectives, and take endings according to the same rules. (See pp. 32, 34, and 35 for full rules and examples.)

Reifere Birnen sind besser.
Riper pears are better.

Der teuerste Hut kostet fünf Mark.*
The *most expensive* hat costs five marks.

Mein ältester Sohn konnte nicht mitkommen.
My *oldest* son could not come along.

In the first sentence, *reifer* is an independent adjective, hence

* *Mark* is invariable, that is, it is not declined, but used in its basic form for all cases and for both singular and plural.

takes *-e* in the nominative plural. *Besser* is a predicate adjective, i.e., it follows the noun it modifies, hence takes no ending.

Teuerste, in the second sentence, is preceded by the definite article, *der*, hence takes *-e* for its masculine, singular, nominative form.

Ältester, in the third sentence, is used after a masculine singular "*ein*-word," hence takes *-er*.

There is one situation in the use of the superlative, however, which is highly idiomatic, and has no counterpart in English. It concerns the manner of expressing a superlative quality idea. There are two ways of expressing this in German:

1. When you use a superlative adjective with a noun, you use the forms we have been discussing up to now, and you treat the superlative exactly like any other adjective.

Die Donau ist der schönst*e* Fluss in Österreich.
The Danube is the most beautiful river in Austria.

2. When you use the superlative adjective as a predicate adjective with the verb *sein* (to be), *bleiben* (to stay or remain), *werden* (to become), or *scheinen* (to appear or seem)—without a noun, or as an adverb—you must use a different form. Add *-n* or *-en* to the ordinary superlative form, and put the word *am* in front of it:

best	best	*am* best*en*	best
schönst	most beautiful	*am* schönst*en*	most beautiful

Die Donau ist *am* schönst*en* in Österreich.
The Danube is *most beautiful* in Austria.

Der Rhein fliesst *am* schnellst*en* in der Schweiz.
The Rhine flows *fastest* in Switzerland.

Making Comparisons

Comparisons are made in much the same way as they are made in English. The English construction *as . . . as* is translated by *so . . . wie.*

Dieser Mann ist *so* alt *wie* mein Bruder.
This man is *as* old *as* my brother.

Than, when used with a comparative adjective, is translated by *als*.

Dieser Mann ist älter *als* mein Bruder.
This man is older *than* my brother.

Adverbs

Adverbs, as in English, do not take declensional endings; they keep the same form no matter how they are used in the sentence. Certain words are always adverbs:

jetzt	now	dort	there
nie	never	bald	soon
nur	only	hier	here

You will find these and others in any dictionary.

Other adverbs, however, are formed from adjectives. Their ordinary or positive form is the same as the adjective itself, but completely without declensional ending:

ADJECTIVE		ADVERB	
schön	beautiful	schön	beautifully
interessant	interesting	interessant	interestingly

Das schön*e*, gemalte Bild . . .   Das *schön* gemalte Bild . . .
The *beautiful*, painted pic-   The *beautifully* painted picture . . .   ture . . .

In the first sentence, *schöne* is an adjective, and has the suitable ending for an adjective following the definite article. In the second sentence, *schön* is an adverb, and therefore takes no ending.

The comparative of adverbs is the same as the comparative of the corresponding adjectives, but again no declensional endings are used:

Diese Eier sind heute *besser* gebraten.
[These eggs are today better fried.]
These eggs are fried better today.

In the superlative, however, only the *am . . . -sten* form (discussed on p. 39) is used:

am schön*sten*	most beautifully
am interessante*sten*	most interestingly
am fein*sten*	most finely

Certain adverbs have irregular comparatives and superlatives:

bald, eher, am ehesten	soon, sooner (rather), soonest
viel, mehr, am meisten	very (much), more, most
gern, lieber, am liebsten	willingly, more willingly, most willingly

Gern lends itself to an idiomatic construction which is discussed below.

The Word "gern"

Gern is a much-used word in German, and can best be translated as *gladly* or *willingly* or as a form of the verb *to like*.

Wir reisen *gern*.	Ich tue es *gern*.
We *like* to travel.	I'll *gladly* do it.

Gern haben is an idiom and means *to like*:

Ich *habe* Sauerkraut *gern*.	Wir *haben* Mathematik *gern*.
I *like* sauerkraut.	We *like* mathematics.

Pronouns

Personal Pronouns

The German personal pronouns are used in much the same way as in English, and to a certain extent correspond to them in form. We shall give only the nominative, dative, and accusative forms. (See p. 113 for the concept and use of cases.)

NOM.		DAT.		ACC.	
ich	I	mir	to me	mich	me
er	he	ihm	" him	ihn	him
sie	she	ihr	" her	sie	her
wir	we	uns	" us	uns	us
sie	they	ihnen	" them	sie	them
Sie	you	Ihnen	" you	Sie	you

Note that *Sie*, the polite form for *you*, is capitalized in all cases. Memorize these forms, for they are very important.

Pronouns follow the same rules for cases as nouns do. The following sentences, which we shall analyze briefly, will demonstrate the use of case.

Können Sie mir ein Zimmer geben, wo ich meinen Hund mitnehmen darf?
[Can you to me a room give, where I my dog take-along may?]
Can you give me a room where I may take my dog along?

Sie is in the nominative since it is the subject of the first clause.
können is plural because *Sie* always takes a plural verb.
mir is dative, since it is the indirect object of *geben*, to give.
ich is nominative, since it is the subject of the second clause.

42

Wenn noch Briefe für mich ankommen, senden Sie sie mir
  bitte nach Karlstadt.
[If any letters for me arrive, send you them to me please to
  Karlstadt.]
If any letters come for me, please send them on to me in
  Karlstadt.

mich is accusative because the preposition *für* takes the accusative.
Sie is nominative since it is the subject of *senden*.
sie is accusative since it is the direct object of *senden*.
mir is dative because it is the indirect object of *senden*.

Ich bin es.
[I am it.]
It is I.

Ich is nominative as the subject of *bin*.   (Observe also that the
German reverses the order of words from the English idiom.)

How to Say "you"

In ordinary conversation, the pronoun *Sie* (including its dative
form, *Ihnen*) is normally used for you. It always takes a plural
verb, whether you are addressing one person or many. It is
always capitalized.

Ich danke *Ihnen* für Ihre Gefälligkeit.
I thank you for your kindness.

Ihnen is dative, since *danken* (to thank) is one of a group of verbs
that take a dative form for an object.
Ihre is a pronoun-adjective meaning *your*. (See p. 28.) It is
also capitalized.
As you probably know from German songs, such as "Du, du
liegst mir im Herzen," there is another word meaning *you* in
German. This is *du* (dative, *dir*; accusative, *dich*). Its plural is
ihr (dative and accusative, *euch*). *Du* and *ihr* are used between
intimate friends, members of the family, with children, and sometimes as an insult. You should learn to recognize these forms

when you hear them, but we advise you not to use them until you know enough German to know which situations call for them.

Relative Pronouns

The most frequently used relative pronoun is very much like the definite article, *der-die-das*. As the following table shows, the two series of forms differ in only five "long forms" from the comparable forms of *der-die-das*.

SINGULAR

	MASC.	FEM.	NEUT.
NOM.	der	die	das
GEN.	*dessen*	*deren*	*dessen*
DAT.	dem	der	dem
ACC.	den	die	das

PLURAL
(all genders)

NOM.	die
GEN.	*deren*
DAT.	*denen*
ACC.	die

The second most common relative pronoun is *welcher*,* which is conjugated like the "*der*-word," *dieser* (see p. 27), except that there are no genitive forms. For genitive forms, you have to use the corresponding forms of *der-die-das*, that is, *dessen, deren, dessen, deren*.

As a general rule, relative pronouns have the same gender and number as the words they stand for, but their case is determined by their function in the sentence. Note especially the examples and the explanations below:

Der Reiseführer, *der* (or *welcher*) uns die Stadt zeigt . . .
[The guide, who us the city shows . . .]
The guide who shows us the city . . .

---

* Do not confuse the relative pronoun *welcher* with the interrogative pronoun or adjective *welcher*. As the interrogative pronoun and adjective, the expected genitive form *wessen* is used.

Der Reiseführer, *dessen* Adresse wir haben wollen, spricht Englisch.

[The guide, whose address we have want, speaks English.]

The guide, whose address we want to have, speaks English.

Der Reiseführer, *dem* (or *welchem*) ich ein gutes Trinkgeld gegeben habe . . .

[The guide, to whom I a good tip given have . . .]

The guide, to whom I gave a good tip . . .

Der Reiseführer, *den* (or *welchen*) ich Ihnen empfehlen kann, heisst Karl Laun.

[The guide, whom I to you recommend can, is called Karl Laun.]

The guide, whom I can recommend to you, is called Karl Laun.

In all of the above sentences, the relative pronouns are masculine singular, because *der Reiseführer*, to which they refer, is a masculine singular noun.

In the first sentence, *der* (or *welcher*) is nominative, because it is the subject of the dependent clause *der uns die Stadt zeigt*.

In the second sentence, *dessen* is genitive because it indicates possession of *Adresse*: the expected genitive form of *welcher* cannot be used, as has been explained above.

In the third sentence, *dem* (or *welchem*) is dative as the indirect object of the verb *gegeben habe*.

In the fourth sentence, *den* (or *welchen*) is accusative as the direct object of the verb *empfehlen*.

You will observe that this use of case closely parallels English.

Word Order after Relative Pronouns

As is explained in the section on word order (p. 87), clauses that are introduced by a relative pronoun require the verb last construction.   In such cases all the verbs go to the end of the clause, with the working verb at the very end.   In such clauses separable verbs (see p. 75) do not split into their components, but remain unified.

Die Strassenbahn, *die* nach dem Schloss fährt, ist Linie drei.

[The streetcar, which to the castle travels, is number three.]

The streetcar which goes to the castle is number three.

Das Auto, *welches* wir gestern gemietet haben, ist ein Volks-
wagen.
[The auto, which we yesterday rented have, is a Volkswagen.]
The auto which we rented yesterday is a Volkswagen.

In the first sentence, *die* is feminine singular because it refers to
die Strassenbahn, which is a feminine noun.

In the second sentence, *welches* is neuter because it refers to *das
Auto*, a neuter noun.

Interrogative Pronouns

The interrogative pronouns *wer* and *was* are declined as follows:

	MASC. and FEM.		NEUT.	
NOM.	wer	who	was	what
GEN.	wessen	whose	wessen	whose, which
DAT.	wem	to whom	—	—
ACC.	wen	who	was	what

The missing dative forms of the neuter *was* are supplied by such
combinations as *womit* (with what), *worauf* (on what), *woran*
(about what), *wodurch* (through what), and *worum* (about what).

Wer hat ein Auto?
Who has a car?

Was hat er gesagt?
[What has he said?]
What did he say?

Wessen Auto ist das?
Whose car is this?

Womit fahren Sie?
[With what travel you?]
How will you travel?

Wem haben Sie meinen Pass
gegeben?
[To whom have you my
passport given?]
To whom have you given my
passport?

Worauf warten Sie?
[On what wait you?]
For what are you waiting?

Wen haben Sie in Frankfurt gesehen?
[Whom have you in Frankfurt seen?]
Whom did you see in Frankfurt?

Prepositions

German prepositions are much more complex in their use than are English prepositions. In English, for instance, we do not have to consider case when using prepositions, except when they are used with pronouns. In German, since the concept of case is much stronger, nouns and pronouns are governed by prepositions which must take definite cases.

There are certain prepositions which always take one and only one case.

GEN. The following prepositions always take the genitive case:

| während | during | anstatt | instead of |
| trotz | in spite of | wegen | on account of |

Während der Nacht konnten wir keinen Wagen finden.
[During the night could we no car find.]
During the night we couldn't find a car.

DAT. The following prepositions always take the dative case:

aus	out of, from	bei	by, near, at
mit	with	nach	after
von	from, of, off	zu	to
seit	since		

Kann ich *mit dem Autobus* fahren?
[Can I with the bus travel?]
Can I go by bus?

Steigen Sie *mit mir* aus, bitte.
[Climb you with me out, please.]
Get off with me, please.

Wo kann ich eine Ansichtspostkarte *von der Stadt* bekommen?
[Where can I a picture post card of the city get?]
Where can I get a picture post card of the city?

Bitte gehen Sie *zu dem Eingang* links.
[Please go you to the entrance left.]
Please go to the entrance to your left.

47

ACC: The following prepositions always take the accusative case:

durch	through	für	for
gegen	against	ohne	without
um	around, about		

Wollen Sie es *für mich* versuchen?
[Will you it for me try?]
Will you try it for me?

Ohne meine Schuhe kann ich nicht ausgehen.
[Without my shoes can I not go out.]
I cannot go out without my shoes.

Other prepositions, however, take more than one case, depending upon their exact meaning. The following prepositions take either the dative or accusative* case:

an	at, on, to	auf	on, upon
hinter	behind	vor	before, in front of
in	in, into	über	over
unter	under, among	zwischen	between
neben	beside		

With these prepositions, the dative case expresses action that takes place in a fixed position or location, while the accusative expresses motion toward or into a place. It is the difference, in exact English, between *in* and *into*, or *on* and *upon*. This is an important distinction in German, and must be observed. Study the examples that follow:

Er stand *an dem* Baum.
He stood *at the* tree. (DAT. since *no* motion is involved.)
Er ging *an den* Baum.
He went *to the* tree. (ACC. since motion is involved.)
Wir sind *in dem* Hause geblieben.
We remained *in the* house. (DAT. since *no* motion is involved.)
Wir sind *in das* Haus gegangen.
We went *into* the house. (ACC. since motion is involved.)

* *An, auf,* and *über,* when used in an abstract sense require the accusative; i.e. *Ich schreibe über meine Reise.* I write about my trip.

Contracted Forms

Prepositions and the definite article are frequently combined into a single word. It is, however, correct to use either the contraction or the two word form. The most common examples are:

an dem *or* am	at the	an das *or* ans	to the
auf das *or* aufs	upon the	bei dem *or* beim	at the
für das *or* fürs	for the	in dem *or* im	in the
in das *or* ins	in the	von dem *or* vom	from, of the
zu dem *or* zum	to the	zu der *or* zur	to the

Prepositions are seldom used with pronouns referring to inanimate objects. Instead, you prefix *da-* (or *dar-* before vowels) to the preposition. This corresponds to our parallel English usage: thereupon, therefore, therewith, etc.

Examples:

Instead of: für ihn, sie, es	Say:	dafür
mit ihm, ihr, ihnen		damit
über ihm, ihr, ihnen *or*		
ihn, sie, es		darüber
auf ihm, ihr, ihnen *or*		
ihn, sie, es		darauf
zu ihm, ihr, ihnen		dazu
in ihm, ihr, ihnen *or*		
ihn, sie, es		darin

Wieviel haben Sie *dafür* bezahlt?
[How much have you there for paid?]
How much did you pay for it?

Simple Verbs

The Present Tense

Although we are usually not aware of it, in English we have three different ways of forming a present tense. We can say *I walk*, or (progressive) *I am walking*, or (emphatic) *I do walk*. There are slight shades of meaning which distinguish these forms. In German, however, there is only one way of expressing present time and only one set of forms to convey all the meanings of the three English forms:

Ich fahre mit dem Zug nach Berlin.
[I travel with the train to Berlin.]
I go (am going) (do go) to Berlin by train.

The word *fahre*, as you have probably observed, means, according to context, I go, I am going, or I do go.

Forming the Present Tense in German

In most cases the present tense of German verbs is formed according to simple and regular rules. As a starting point take the infinitive of the verb, just as you do in English:

sagen   to say   reden   to speak

This form is used as a basis for all forms of the present. As you notice, it ends in *-en*, or less commonly, in *-n*. The present tense is then made as follows:

SINGULAR

ich sag*e*	I say	ich red*e*	I speak
er sag*t*	he says	er rede*t*	he speaks
sie sag*t*	she says	sie rede*t*	she speaks
es sag*t*	it says	es rede*t*	it speaks

50

PLURAL

wir sagen	we say	wir reden	we speak
sie sagen	they say	sie reden	they speak
Sie sagen	you say	Sie reden	you speak

1. All the plural forms, including *Sie* (*you*, even if referring to only one person) are exactly the same as the infinitive. This is true of every verb in the German language, with only one exception: *sein* (to be). We shall discuss *sein* separately, since it is very irregular (see p. 52).

2. All the *I* forms (first person singular) drop the *-en* or *-n* of the infinitive, and add *-e*. This rule is true of almost all verbs, although there is a very frequently used group of verbs like *can, must, may*, etc. which are irregular and which we shall discuss separately (p. 67).

3. All the *he-she-it* forms (third person singular) drop the *-en* or *-n* of the infinitive, and add *-t*. This rule has exceptions:

(a) the words for *can, may, shall, must, will, is, has*, etc., which we shall consider separately.

(b) A very important group of verbs which make this change, but also change the vowel in their stem. These are called stem-changing verbs, and shall be described immediately.

(c) In verbs whose stem ends in *d* or *t*, a connective-e-is inserted between stem and ending. Note red*et* above.

Forming the Present Tense of Stem-changing Verbs

Some verbs, besides adding *-t* to their stem to form the *he-she-it* forms of the present tense, also change the vowel in the stem. In such cases an *a* in the stem is changed to *ä*, and *e* is changed to either *i* or *ie*, depending upon the individual verb. Three common verbs of this sort are:

SINGULAR

a TO ä		e TO ie	
fahren	to travel	sehen	to see
ich fahre	I travel	ich sehe	I see
er fährt	he travels	er sieht	he sees
sie fährt	she travels	sie sieht	she sees
es fährt	it travels	es sieht	it sees

e TO i

geben	to give
ich gebe	I give
er g*i*bt	he gives
sie g*i*bt	she gives
es g*i*bt*	it gives

Note: There are no stem changes in the plural.

There is no way to identify such stem-changing verbs beyond the fact that they are all strong verbs (see p. 54 for a definition of a strong verb). You must either memorize them or consult a dictionary when you are in doubt. Most dictionaries and grammars indicate these verbs either by quoting such forms in full, or by some such notation as *sehen* (*ie*), plus the vowel changes in the past tense and in the past participle.

The Verbs "to be" and "to have"

The verbs *sein* (to be) and *haben* (to have) are as commonly used in German as their counterparts are in English. Besides their use as words by themselves, they are also used to form other verb forms, in much the same manner as they are in English. (See pp. 56 and 58 for their use as auxiliary verbs.)

It will prove a great help to you if you practice these forms until they become as automatic as their English equivalents.

PRESENT TENSE
sein (to be)

ich bin	I am	wir sind	we are
er ist	he is	sie sind	they are
sie ist	she is	Sie sind	you are
es ist	it is		

haben (to have)

ich habe	I have	wir haben	we have
er hat	he has	sie haben	they have
sie hat	she has	Sie haben	you have
es hat	it has		

* As an idiom, *es gibt* means "there is" or "there are."

PAST TENSE

sein (to be)

ich war	I was	wir waren	we were
er war	he was	sie waren	they were
sie war	she was	Sie waren	you were
es war	it was		

haben (to have)

ich hatte	I had	wir hatten	we had
er hatte	he had	sie hatten	they had
sie hatte	she had	Sie hatten	you had
es hatte	it had		

Observe that you have to memorize only two or three forms for each tense of these two verbs. Also notice how close these forms resemble their corresponding English forms.

Wo *ist* die Wäscherei?
Where *is* the laundry?

Ich *habe* einen internationalen Führerschein.
I *have* an international driver's licence.

Haben Sie ein Zimmer frei?
[Have you a room vacant?]
Do you *have* a vacant room?

The Past Participle

One of the basic forms of the German verb which you must learn is the past participle. It is sometimes used as an adjective, as in English, but its most frequent use is to form the perfect tenses, as in English. In the English sentence "I have not eaten since breakfast," *eaten* is a past participle.

In English, as you will notice, if you run mentally through a few verbs, there are two ways of forming the past participle. Some verbs, like learn, walk, live, fear, and laugh form their past participle by adding -*d* or -*ed* to the basic form: learn*ed*, walk*ed*, liv*ed*, fear*ed*, laugh*ed*. These are called weak verbs.

Other verbs, however, form their past participles in a more complex way. Take the English verbs find, sing, swim, speak, and drink. They form their past participles respectively as found, sung, swum, spoken, and drunk. The points that they have in common are (1) they do not add -d or -ed to form their past participle, and (2) they change the vowel in their stem. These are called strong verbs.

In German exactly the same situation exists. There are strong verbs and there are weak verbs. And, as in English, there are a few irregular verbs.

How to Tell a Strong Verb from a Weak Verb

Unfortunately, there is no simple rule to aid you in identifying strong or weak verbs. However, comparable verbs in English frequently furnish valuable information for you.

For example, if there is an English verb which is closely related to the German verb—as *live* is to *leben*, *see* is to *sehen*, *drink* is to *trinken*, *find* is to *finden*—in most cases the German verb will be strong if the English cognate is strong. This is, however, not always the case, and it is safer (1) to memorize the past participle of a verb when you learn the verb, and (2) to get into the habit of looking up unfamiliar forms in your dictionary.

Forming the Past Participle of Weak Verbs

German weak verbs form their past participles very simply. They add -t (or -et if the stem ends in *d* or *t*) and they add *ge-* to the front of the verb stem. (Those exceptional verbs which do not add *ge-* are discussed on pp. 55–56.)

INFINITIVE		PAST PARTICIPLE	
lernen	to learn	*ge*lern*t*	learned
antworten	to answer	*ge*antwort*et*	answered
leben	to live	*ge*leb*t*	lived
sagen	to say	*ge*sag*t*	said

Forming the Past Participle of Strong Verbs

German strong verbs, like English verbs, are more difficult to analyze. They

1. retain the original ending of the infinitive (-n or -en)
2. prefix ge-
3. usually change the vowel in the stem of the verb.

INFINITIVE		PAST PARTICIPLE	
finden	to find	*gefunden*	found
sehen	to see	*gesehen*	seen
tun	to do	*getan*	done
sprechen	to speak	*gesprochen*	spoken
trinken	to drink	*getrunken*	drunk
scheinen	to shine	*geschienen*	shone

There are no simple rules for determining what sound changes are made in the vowels of German past participles, just as there are no simple rules in English. Memorize the past participle forms or else look them up in a dictionary.

There are also a few frequently used verbs (strong or weak) which, like their English counterparts, form irregular past participles:

INFINITIVE		PAST PARTICIPLE	
sein	to be	gewesen	been
stehen	to stand	gestanden	stood
gehen	to go	gegangen	gone
bringen	to bring	gebracht	brought
denken	to think	gedacht	thought
essen	to eat	gegessen	eaten
sitzen	to sit	gesessen	sat

Some Exceptions

A group of irregular weak verbs borrowed from the Romance languages do not prefix a ge- to the verb stem to form the past participle, but do add a final *-t*. The infinitives of these verbs all end in *-ieren*. Examples:

INFINITIVE		PAST PARTICIPLE	
reservieren	to reserve	reserviert	reserved
amüsieren	to amuse	amüsiert	amused
spazieren	to walk	spaziert	walked

Important Note: All the rules and procedures which we have discussed in this section apply only to simple verbs. Separable verbs and inseparable verbs (for which see respectively pp. 75 and 79) form their past participles in a slightly different manner. For ease of learning, however, review the rules for forming the past participles of simple verbs first. Later, when you study separable and inseparable verbs, you will see that forming their past participles involves only slight modification of these rules.

The Conversational Past Tense

The most frequently used past tense in German is the conversational past, which corresponds in formation to the English present perfect tense. As in English, it is formed with the past participle and an auxiliary verb.

Er *hat* hier ein Zimmer für uns *reserviert.*

[He *has* here a room for us *reserved.*]

He reserved (or has reserved) a room for us here.

In English, *has reserved* is present perfect tense, and *hat reserviert* in German is conversational past or present perfect tense. Observe that *hat reserviert* does not have to be translated as *has reserved*; it can mean simply *reserved.*

In modern English we form all present perfect tenses by using forms of the verb *to have* and the past participle of a verb. Most German verbs follow the same pattern, using forms of the verb *haben* (to have) and a past participle:

ich habe gesehen	I saw; I have seen
er, sie, es hat gefunden	he, she, it found; he, she, it has found

| wir haben gesagt | we said; we have said |
| sie, Sie haben gekauft | they, you bought; they, you have bought |

Der Kellner *hat* einen guten Wein *gebracht.*
[The waiter *has* a good wine *brought.*]
The waiter brought a good wine.

Danke, ich *habe* genug *gesehen.*
[Thank you, I *have* enough *seen.*]
Thank you, I have seen enough.

Observe that the past participle is placed at the end of these sentences, and that German follows a characteristic word order in sentences that contain perfect forms.   You will find this important point explained in detail on p. 85.

Most German verbs make their conversational past tense by using *haben* as their auxiliary or working verb. Some verbs, however, do not use *haben*, but use, instead, forms of *sein* (to be).

ich bin gegangen	I went; I have gone
sie, er, es ist gestorben	she, he, it died; she, he, it has died
wir sind geblieben	we remained; we have remained
sie, Sie sind gefallen	they, you fell; they, you have fallen

Die Teller *sind* kalt *gewesen.*
[The plates *are* cold *been.*]
The plates were cold.

Meine Frau und Tochter *sind* allein *ausgegangen.*
[My wife and daughter *are* alone *out-gone.*]
My wife and daughter *went out* alone.

This may seem to be a strange usage, but actually English made use of forms exactly like these until only a few centuries ago. The King James Bible, for example, uses such forms as I *am* come, Christ *is* risen, Babylon the Great *is* fallen.

"Haben" and "sein" as Auxiliary Verbs

Any German verb which takes a direct object must use *haben* to form its conversational past and other perfect tenses. This includes ordinary transitive verbs, reflexive verbs, and most impersonal verbs. Most intransitive verbs and most modal verbs also use *haben* to form perfect tenses.

Only three categories of German verbs use *sein* as an auxiliary. These are:

1. Verbs involving a change of position that cannot take an object.

INFINITIVE		CONVERSATIONAL PAST	
kommen	to come	ich bin gekommen	I came; I have come
gehen	to go	ich bin gegangen	I went; I have gone
fahren	to travel	wir sind gefahren	we travelled; we have travelled
fallen	to fall	es ist gefallen	it fell; it has fallen
steigen	to climb	sie ist gestiegen	she climbed; she has climbed
folgen	to follow	er ist mir gefolgt	he followed me; he has followed me

2. Verbs involving a change of condition that cannot take an object.

wachsen	to grow	ich bin gewachsen	I grew; I have grown
sterben	to die	er ist gestorben	he died; he has died
verschwinden	to disappear	sie ist verschwunden	she disappeared; she has disappeared

3. Miscellaneous verbs

sein	to be	wir sind gewesen	we were; we have been

bleiben	to remain	er ist geblieben	he remained; he has remained
werden	to become	ich bin geworden	I became; I have become
gelingen	to succeed	es ist ihm gelungen	he succeeded; he has succeeded
geschehen	to happen	es ist geschehen	it happened; it has happened

If you find it difficult to remember these categories, memorize a complete perfect form when you learn a verb, or else consult the dictionary. Most dictionaries will show "aux. *h*." for *haben* or "aux. *s*." for *sein* to indicate the proper auxiliary.

How to Form the Simple Past Tense

You have already learned the conversational past tense, which corresponds in form to the English perfect or present perfect tense. You should also learn the German simple past tense, which corresponds in form to the English simple past.

German verbs, like English verbs, fall into two large categories: weak verbs and strong verbs. Weak verbs in both languages do not change their stem vowel in forming their simple past tense. Strong verbs in both languages do change their stem vowels. (See pp. 53–54 for discussion of strong and weak verbs.)

German weak verbs form their simple past by adding the letter *-t* to the stem of the verb, plus the ending *-e* in the singular, and *-en* in the plural. English corresponding forms are live, lived; walk, walked; grasp, grasped, etc.

SING.	leben (to live)		PL.
ich leb*te*	I lived	wir leb*ten*	we lived
er leb*te*	he lived	sie leb*ten*	they lived
sie leb*te*	she lived	Sie leb*ten*	you lived
es leb*te*	it lived		

SING. antworten (to answer) PL.

ich antwort*ete*	I answered	wir antwort*eten*	we answered
er antwort*ete*	he answered	sie antwort*eten*	they answered
sie antwort*ete*	she answered	Sie antwort*eten*	you answered
es antwort*ete*	it answered		

Observe that a connective -*e*- has been added between the stem and the endings of the verb *antworten*. This is done with verbs whose stem ends in -*d* or -*t*, to make the past tense audibly distinct.

German strong verbs form their simple past tense by changing their stem vowel; no ending is added to the singular forms, while -*en* is used for the plural forms. You are familiar with similar vowel changes in English strong verbs: swim, swam; give, gave; take, took; strive, strove; see, saw, etc.

SING. geben (to give) PL.

ich gab	I gave	wir gaben	we gave
er gab	he gave	sie gaben	they gave
sie gab	she gave	Sie gaben	you gave
es gab	it gave		

kommen (to come)

ich kam	I came	wir kamen	we came
er kam	he came	sie kamen	they came
sie kam	she came	Sie kamen	you came
es kam	it came		

See p. 97 for a list of the more common strong verbs.

How to Use the Simple Past Tense

On the whole, the simple past tense and the conversational past in German are interchangeable:

Was haben Sie gesagt? (conversational past)
What have you said? What did you say?

Was sagten Sie? (simple past)
[What said you?]
What did you say? What have you said?

Where English uses a past progressive tense (see p. 108), however, you should use the simple past tense in German.

Als wir Kaffee tranken, gaben wir dem Kellner ein Trinkgeld.
[When we coffee were drinking, gave we to the waiter a tip.]
When we were drinking coffee, we gave the waiter a tip.

Commands

Commands are normally expressed by taking the *Sie* form of the present tense of the verb, and placing the verb before the pronoun *Sie*.

Kommen Sie herein und *schliessen Sie* die Tür!
[Come you in and shut you the door!]
Come in and shut the door!

Observe that the pronoun *Sie* is repeated if two or more commands are given in the same sentence.

Negative commands are made in the same way as positive commands, with the appropriate negative adverbs and adjectives. German does not have a construction exactly parallel to the English *Do not* . . .

Bestellen Sie bitte heute keinen Kaffee!
[Order you please today no coffee!]
Please don't order coffee today!

The usual word for please, *bitte*, does not change, any more than does its English equivalent.

Observe that word order for commands is like that for questions. In conversation, however, a question is spoken with a rising inflection of the voice, as in English.

Verbs with "du" and "ihr"

As has been explained on p. 43, there is another way of saying *you* besides the polite form, *Sie*. This is the familiar personal pronoun: *du*, singular; *ihr*, plural. We do not advise you to use these forms until you know the situations that call for them, but we include them so that you will recognize them. As a general rule, *du* takes a verb form that is closely related to the Old English *thou* form—thou seest, thou doest, etc. In present tenses, the *du* form is made by dropping the *t* of the he-she-it form, and adding, instead, *-st*. As this implies, if the verb is a stem-changing verb, the *du* form uses the changed vowel.

INFIN.		SECOND PERSON SING.	
haben	to have	du ha*st*	you have
sehen	to see	du sieh*st*	you see

The following verbs have irregular forms in the present tense:

INFIN.		SECOND PERSON SING.	
werden	to become	du wirst	you become
(auxiliary for the future tense)			
sein	to be	du bist	you are
wissen	to know	du weisst	you know
müssen	to have to	du musst	you have to
wollen	to want to	du willst	you want to
können	to be able	du kannst	you are able

In the simple past, you add *-st* to the he-she-it form:

INFIN.		THIRD PERSON SING.	
kaufen	to buy	er kaufte	he bought
kommen	to come	er kam	he came

SECOND PERSON SING.

du kauft*est*	you bought
du kam*st*	you came

The plural of *du* is *ihr*, which should not be confused with *ihr* the dative form of *sie* (she). Its verb form is made by taking the third person plural of the verb concerned, dropping the *-n* (or *-en*) and adding *-(e)t*. As you can see, it is often identical with the third person singular.

To form the past tense, add *-et* to the past stem of all weak and strong verbs whose stem ends in *-d* or *-t*; add *-t* to all others.

PRESENT TENSE

SECOND PERSON SING. AND PL. (polite)		SECOND PERSON PL. (familiar)	
Sie kaufen	you buy	ihr kauf*t*	you buy
Sie arbeiten	you work	ihr arbeit*et*	you work
Sie sind	you are	ihr *seid*	you are (irregular)

SIMPLE PAST TENSE

Sie kauften	you bought	ihr kauft*et*	you bought
Sie arbeiteten	you worked	ihr arbeite*tet*	you worked
Sie waren	you were	ihr war*t*	you were

How to Form the Future Tense

The future tense in German is made by using the present tense of the verb *werden* with the infinitive of the verb concerned in the sentence. The German future corresponds, as you can see, almost exactly with the English use of *shall* and *will* (plus an infinitive) to form the future. Note that *werden* is an irregular verb.

SING.	gehen (to go)	PL.	
ich werde gehen	I shall go	wir werden gehen	we shall go
er wird gehen	he will go	sie werden gehen	they will go
sie wird gehen	she will go	Sie werden gehen	you will go
es wird gehen	it will go		

Ich werde heute nach Hause zurückkommen.
[I shall today to home back-come.]
I shall return home today.

Werden Sie einen Platz für mich auf dem Flugzeug reservieren?
[Will you a place for me on the airplane reserve?]
Will you reserve a place for me on the airplane?

Observe that in these independent sentences in the future tense, the infinitive is placed at the very end (see p. 85).

You can often avoid using the future tense by using the present tense with an indication of time.

Ich gehe heute abend ins Theater.
[I am going today evening into the theatre.]
I am going to the theatre tonight.

As you have probably observed, this corresponds to English usage, i.e., the present tense is used to indicate a future action with the help of *tonight*.

Reflexive Verbs and Reflexive Pronouns

Reflexive verbs in German use the following pronouns, which correspond in general to the English pronouns ending in -*self*:

mich or mir*	myself
sich	himself, herself, itself, oneself, yourself, themselves, yourselves
uns	ourselves

These pronouns are called reflexive pronouns, and the verbs that use them are called reflexive verbs. In English we use such reflexive verbs occasionally (I washed myself. He locked himself out. We found ourselves late, etc.), but German uses them more often, and in situations where we do not use them. They are indicated in dictionaries by such abbreviations as *refl.* or *rf.* or by the presence of the pronoun with the infinitive: *sich freuen* (to rejoice).

Reflexive verbs are conjugated like other verbs, and all use *haben* in forming their conversational past tense. The reflexive pronoun is placed in the sentence exactly as if it were an object pronoun (which in a way it is).

sich setzen (to sit down)

ich setze mich	I sit down	wir setzen uns	we sit down
er setzt sich	he sits down	sie setzen sich	they sit down
sie setzt sich	she sits down	Sie setzen sich	you sit down
es setzt sich	it sits down		

* See p. 65 for discussion on how to use *mir*.

Können *Sie sich* nicht an ihn *erinnern?*
[Can *you yourself* not about him *remember?*]
Can't you remember him?

Ich *habe mich geirrt,* aber *ich will mich bessern.*
[I *have myself erred,* but *I want-to myself improve.*]
I have made a mistake, but I want to improve.

As we observed in the first paragraph of this section, two forms
are given for myself: *mich* and *mir.*   *Mich* is the form ordinarily
used, but in certain verbs where the word *myself* conveys the idea
to myself or *for myself, mir* is used.   You should memorize these
important verbs that take *mir*:

sich denken	to imagine
sich Sorge machen um etwas	to worry about something
sich weh tun	to hurt oneself

Ich denke es *mir.*
I imagine it.

Ich mache *mir* Sorgen um etwas.
I worry about something.

Ich tue *mir* weh.
I hurt myself.

Observe the use of *mir* in the following examples:

Ich kaufe *mir* ein Buch.
I buy myself a book

Ich lasse *mir* das Haar schneiden.
[I have myself the hair cut.]
I have my hair cut.

Note 1. Observe that *sich,* the reflexive pronoun meaning yourself or yourselves is not capitalized, even though *Sie* is.

Note 2. Do not confuse the -self pronouns used with reflexive
verbs with such expressions as I, myself; you, yourself, etc.   These
use a different form, *selbst,* which does not change.

Sie haben es *selbst* gesagt.
[You have it *yourself* said.]
You yourself said it.

Forming the Passive Voice

The same auxiliary verb which was used to form the future tense (see p. 63) is also used to form the passive voice in German. This is the verb *werden* (to become). The present passive is formed by using the present tense of *werden* with the past participle of the verb concerned, and the past passive is formed by using the past tense of *werden* with the past participle of the verb.

PRESENT TENSE of WERDEN

ich werde	I become	wir werden	we become
er wird	he becomes	sie werden	they become
sie wird	she becomes	Sie werden	you become
es wird	it becomes		

PAST TENSE of WERDEN

ich wurde	I became	wir wurden	we became
er wurde	he became	sie wurden	they became
sie wurde	she became	Sie wurden	you became
es wurde	it became		

Examples of passive voice:

Meine Uhr *wird* von ihm *gereinigt.*
[My watch *becomes* by him *cleaned.*]
My watch is being cleaned by him.

Das Buch *wurde* von meiner Frau *gekauft.*
[The book *became* by my wife *bought.*]
The book was bought by my wife.

Observe that the past participle has been placed at the end of these two sentences, just as in the perfect tenses. It follows the same rules for placement (see p. 85). Also notice that *by* in passive sentences is usually translated by *von*, less often by *durch*.

How to Avoid the Passive Voice

The German passive voice is often considered difficult by Americans, and, indeed, in perfect tenses it can be complex. Actually, as in English, there are very few ideas that demand a passive sentence; most concepts can be expressed just as well by re-wording your thought to an active form. The two sentences in the preceding section, for example, could just as well be expressed as "He is cleaning my watch" and "My wife bought this book."

Another way to avoid the passive voice is to use the pronoun *man* to express the same idea. *Man* is an impersonal pronoun which is used when no specific reference is intended; it corresponds to the impersonal *you* or impersonal *they* or *one* in comparable English sentences: you may smoke in the lobby, they say it will be a cold winter, one does not often hear such fine playing. Thus, the passive voice in the sentence

Diese Strasse wurde letztes Jahr gebaut.
[This street was last year built.]
This street was built last year.

can be avoided by saying:

Man hat diese Strasse letztes Jahr gebaut.
[One has this street last year built.]
They built this street last year.

Expressing "Must," "Can" and "Want to"

The German words which correspond to the English must, can, and want to are irregular in many of their forms. Since they are just as common in German as in English, they should be memorized.

This is their present tense:

müssen (expressing the idea must, have to, etc.)

ich muss	I must	wir müssen	we must
er muss	he must	sie müssen	they must
sie muss	she must	Sie müssen	you must
es muss	it must		

wollen (expressing the idea want to, would like to, etc.)

ich will	I want to	wir wollen	we want to
er will	he wants to	sie wollen	they want to
sie will	she wants to	Sie wollen	you want to
es will	it wants to		

können (expressing the idea can, is able to, etc.)

ich kann	I can	wir können	we can
er kann	he can	sie können	they can
sie kann	she can	Sie können	you can
es kann	it can		

Observe that in all three of these verbs, all the singular forms are the same, for each verb, and all the plural forms are the same. You have to memorize only two forms for the present tense of each verb.

These three verbs take the infinitive of the complementary verb, exactly as their counterparts do in English.   Observe that the infinitive is placed at the end of the clause (see p. 85 for the general rule).

Ich will meine Wäsche *trocknen.*
[*I want-to* my wash *dry.*]
I want to dry my wash.

Wir können die Musik nicht *hören.*
[*We can* the music not *hear.*]
We cannot hear the music.

Er muss sich jetzt *ausruhen.*
[*He must* himself now *rest.*]
He must rest now.

Observe that the word *zu* is not used with these verbs.   They are followed directly by the infinitive, without *zu.*   This corresponds to English usage with the comparable words can, could, should, would, must, etc.

The past tense of these verbs is formed in the following manner:

müssen (must, have to, etc.)

ich musste	I had to	wir mussten	we had to
er musste	he had to	sie mussten	they had to
sie musste	she had to	Sie mussten	you had to
es musste	it had to		

Wollen (to wish to) and *können* (to be able to) follow the same pattern of having all singular forms identical and all plural forms identical:

SINGULAR		PLURAL	
wollte	wanted to	wollten	wanted to
konnte	could	konnten	could

Herr Schmidt konnte die Post nicht finden.
[Mr. Schmidt could the post office not find.]
Mr. Schmidt could not find the post office.

Wir mussten ihm den Schlüssel geben.
[We had-to to him the key give.]
We had to give him the key.

Sie wollten ihn nicht treffen.
[They wanted-to him not meet.]
They did not want to meet him.

The future of these three verbs, *müssen, können,* and *wollen,* is entirely regular, and is formed with *werden,* just as is the future tense of all other verbs.   (See p. 63 for a full statement about the future of all verbs.)

Ich werde nicht kommen *können.*
[I shall not to come *to be able.*]
I shall not be able to come.

As you have probably noticed, there are two infinitives in the sentence, *kommen* and *können.*   In such cases *können* or *müssen* or *wollen* is placed immediately after the other infinitive, as in the above example.

Would and Should

In English there are many situations where we use the words should or would with an infinitive. These situations indicate hope, belief, desire, indirect questions, indirect statements, and conditions. (See the examples below.) In most cases it is possible to translate these sentences into German, almost word for word, by using the words *würde* or *würden* with an infinitive: *würde* is used for singular forms; *würden* for plural forms.

ich würde gehen	I would go
er würde kommen	he would come
sie würde sehen	she would see
es würde geschehen	it would happen
wir würden schreiben	we would write
sie würden lesen	they would read
Sie würden bezahlen	you would pay

Ich hatte gehofft, Sie *würden* mir ein Zimmer *reservieren.*
[I had hoped, you *would* for me a room *reserve.*]
I had hoped you would reserve a room for me.

Meine Frau wünscht, Frau Schmidt *würde* bald *schreiben.*
[My wife wishes, Mrs. Schmidt *would* soon *write.*]
My wife wishes Mrs. Schmidt would write soon.

Ich *würde* das nicht *sagen.*
[I *would* that not *to say.*]
I wouldn't say so.

Der Arzt sagte, er *würde* uns *telefonieren.*
[The doctor said, he *would* us *telephone.*]
The doctor said he would telephone us.

Wenn es billiger wäre, so *würde* ich es *kaufen.*
[If it cheaper were, so *would* I it *buy.*]
If it were cheaper, I would buy it.

Wir haben nicht geglaubt, dass Sie uns *verstehen würden.*
[We have not believed, that you us *understand would.*]
We didn't believe that you would understand us.

Die alte Dame fragte, ob es *regnen würde.*

[The old lady asked, whether it *rain would.*]

The old lady asked whether it would rain.

Observe the word order in the sentences, particularly that of the infinitives. The infinitives *reservieren, schreiben, sagen, telefonieren,* and *kaufen* are all at the end of their statements because they are in independent clauses (see p. 85). The infinitives *verstehen* and *regnen,* however, are in dependent clauses, and for this reason come before the working verbs *würden* and *würde.*

It must be noted that the word *should* is sometimes used in English with the pronouns I and we to express the same ideas as *would* in the above examples. Colloquially, we say, "If it were cheaper, I would buy it," but in writing we might also say, "If it were cheaper, I should buy it." *Should,* in these cases, does not mean *ought to* or *must.* When should means *ought to* or *must,* it is expressed differently in German. Singular forms use *sollte* with the infinitive; plural forms use *sollten* with the infinitive.

Er *sollte* nicht so spät *aufbleiben.*

[*He should* so late not *stay-up.*]

He should not stay up so late.   He ought not to stay up so late.

Sie sollten sich Ihr Geld *sparen.*

[*You ought* yourself your money *save.*]

You ought to save your money.

Würde and *würden* are what is technically known as forms of the imperfect subjunctive of *werden* (to become), the same verb that you have used to form the future and the passive. By using *würde* and *würden* as indicated above, you will be able to express most of the ideas normally conveyed by the rather complex subjunctive forms for other verbs.

Impersonal Verbs

German, like English, has many impersonal verbs. Some of them correspond rather closely to English:

es schneit   it snows, it is snowing

es regnet   it rains, it is raining
es geschieht   it happens, it is happening

Impersonal verbs are used more commonly in German, however, and there are many German impersonal constructions that do not have English counterparts. Some of the most common of these German impersonal constructions are:

Es tut mir leid.
[It does to me sorrow.]
I am sorry.

Es gelingt ihm, seinen Freund zu erreichen.
[It succeeds to him his friend to reach.]
He succeeds in contacting his friend.

Es gefällt mir.
It pleases me.

Es fehlt mir die Zeit dazu.
[It lacks to me the time to this.]
I don't have time for that.

Wie geht es Ihnen?   Es geht mir gut.
[How goes it to you?   It goes to me good.]
How are you?   Good.

Es sind drei Männer im ersten Abteil.
There are three men in the first compartment.

Es fällt mir schwer.
[It falls me heavy.]
It is hard for me.   I find it hard.

Es geht mir schlecht.
[It goes to me bad.]
Things are not well with me.

Es ist mir übel.
[It is to me sick.]
I feel sick.   I feel nauseated.

Verbs that Take Their Objects in the Dative Case

Most German verbs use the accusative for their direct objects (see p. 96). There are a few very common verbs, however, which do not use the accusative, but the dative.

antworten (to answer)
Antworten Sie *ihm*!
Answer him!

danken (to thank)
Wir haben *ihm* gedankt.
We thanked him.

folgen (to follow)
Wir folgen *dem Reiseführer*.
We follow the travel guide.

gefallen (to please, to like)
Diese Stadt gefällt *mir*.
[This town pleases *me*.]
I like this town.

gehören (to belong to)
Der Koffer gehört *meiner Frau*.
The suitcase belongs to my wife.

glauben (to believe)
Ich glaube *ihr*.
I believe her.

helfen (to help)
Helfen Sie *mir*!
Help me!

Compound Verbs

Prefixes and Verbs
(Compound Verbs)

All the verbs which you have studied up to now have been simple verbs. That is to say, they are one unit, without prefixes.

In German, however, just as in English, new verbs conveying new or expanded ideas are made by combining such simple verbs with prefixes. In English, for example, we have as simple verbs: to take, to come, to go, and to say. From these are made: to undertake, to overtake, to mistake, to retake, to overcome, to become, to welcome, to undergo, to gainsay, and similar new words. In German the same phenomenon takes place on a larger and more complex scale.

geben	to give
angeben	to declare
aufgeben	to give up
ausgeben	to distribute, give out, spend
sich begeben	to go, set out for, happen
vorgeben	to pretend, allege
übergeben	to hand over, to vomit
vergeben	to forgive

One great difference exists, however, between these German forms and their English relatives. In English, verbs built out of simple verbs and prefixes are used exactly like other verbs and present no special problems. In German, on the other hand, compound verbs behave differently from simple verbs, and you must master their use before you speak correct German. Even though this use may be somewhat difficult for you at first, it must be learned.

There are two groups of compound verbs:

1. verbs formed with prefixes which can be detached from the verb. These are called separable verbs.

2. verbs formed with prefixes that cannot be detached. These

74

are called inseparable verbs. We shall consider each group separately.

Separable Verbs

The first group of compound verbs which you should learn to use are the so-called separable verbs. They are called separable because in certain situations (which we shall discuss below) the prefix and the verb itself become separated from one another.

In quite a few cases you can tell a separable verb by its prefix. If a verb has one of the following prefixes it is separable:

(examples)

PREFIX	BASIC VERB	SEPARABLE VERB
ab	nehmen	abnehmen
(off)	(to take)	(to take off)
an	sehen	ansehen
(at, on)	(to see)	(to view)
auf	stehen	aufstehen
(up)	(to stand)	(to stand up)
aus	gehen	ausgehen
(out)	(to go)	(to go out)
bei	bringen	beibringen
(by, with, at)	(to bring)	(to teach)
ein	laden	einladen
(in, into)	(to load)	(to invite)
empor	heben	emporheben
(up)	(to lift)	(to lift up)
fort	gehen	fortgehen
(away)	(to go)	(to go away)
heim	kommen	heimkommen
(home)	(to come)	(to return home)
her	stellen	herstellen
(hither, here)	(to place)	(to manufacture)
hin	fahren	hinfahren
(thither, away)	(to travel)	(to travel, sail to)
los	lassen	loslassen
(loose)	(to let)	(to release)

(examples)

PREFIX	BASIC VERB	SEPARABLE VERB
mit	nehmen	mitnehmen
(with)	(to take)	(to take along)
nach	lassen	nachlassen
(after)	(to let)	(to slacken)
nieder	reissen	niederreissen
(down)	(to tear)	(to tear down)
vor	ziehen	vorziehen
(before)	(to pull)	(to prefer)
weg	gehen	weggehen
(away)	(to go)	(to go away)
zu	machen	zumachen
(to)	(to make)	(to close)
zurück	bleiben	zurückbleiben
(back)	(to remain)	(to remain behind)

Separable verbs make the same changes to indicate tenses and persons as their original parent verbs. If the original parent verb is a weak verb, the separable verbs that are formed from it will be weak. If the original verb is a strong verb, the separable verbs made from it will make the same stem changes as the parent verb, and will be strong. For example, *abnehmen* (to take off) is derived from *nehmen*, to take, which has as its simple past *nahm*, and its past participle *genommen*. *Abnehmen* will make the same changes. The difference between separable verbs and simple verbs lies not in endings and stem changes, but in the position of the prefix in the sentence.

How Separable and Simple Verbs Differ

The position of separable verbs differs from simple verbs in three situations: (1) the present tense, the simple past, the command forms, (2) the past participle, and (3) the infinitive with *zu*. We shall describe each of these in detail.

Difference 1. In the present tense, the simple past, and the command forms, the prefix and the verb separate in all situations *except* in clauses where transposed word order is used. (See Rule 4, under word order, p. 87). The verb stays in its normal place in the sentence, while the prefix is placed at the very end of the clause.

Ich *nehme* meinen Hut *ab*.
[I *take* my hat *off*.]
I take off my hat.

Nehmen Sie die Einladung *an*?
[*Take you* the invitation *on*?]
Are you accepting the invitation?

Geben Sie mir mein Geld *zurück*, bitte.
[*Give* you to me my money *back*, please.]
Give me back my money, please.

If, on the other hand, the separable verb is in a clause that is using transposed word order (Rule 4), the prefix and the verb *do not* separate, and the separable verb is treated exactly like an ordinary simple verb.

Wenn ich meinen Hut *abnehme*, werde ich mich erkälten.
[If I my hat *off-take*, shall I myself catch-a-cold.]
If I take my hat off, I shall catch a cold.

Als wir die Einladung *annahmen*, waren wir in Hamburg.
[When we the invitation *accepted*, were we in Hamburg.]
When we accepted the invitation, we were in Hamburg.

As you will observe, the first clause in both of the above examples is in transposed word order because the clauses begin, respectively, with *wenn* and *als*, which take this word order. The second clause of each sentence is in inverted word order (Rule 3, p. 86), because the first element in the sentence is not the subject (*ich* and *wir*), but rather the two first clauses.

Difference 2. To form the past participle of separable verbs, *-ge-* is used, as in most simple verbs, but it is placed between the prefix and the verb itself. This compound is never broken.

This past participle is used for exactly the same purposes as the past participle of a simple verb.

abnehmen   to take off   abgenommen   taken off

Wir haben unsre Hüte *abgenommen.*
[We have our hats *off-taken.*]
We took off our hats.   We have taken off our hats.

Difference 3. When *zu* is used with the infinitive of separable verbs, *-zu-* is placed between the prefix and the verb proper, and the three parts form a single word:

Um Bilder des Waldes *aufzunehmen,* müssen Sie am Fluss entlanggehen.
[In order pictures of the forest *to take,* must you the river along go.]
In order to take pictures of the forest, you must go along the river.

In all other circumstances, separable verbs are treated exactly like their parent verbs, and prefix and verb proper are not separated.

Der Kellner wird uns drei Glas Bier *herausbringen.*
[The waiter will us three glasses of beer *out-here-bring.*]
The waiter will serve us three glasses of beer out here.

Since the prefixes of separable verbs are placed at the end of the clause in some occasions, you must get in the habit of waiting for the end of the clause before deciding what the verb means. Such prefixes at the end of the clause may change the meaning of the verb considerably from the meaning of the simple verb form that you met in the earlier part of the sentence.

Man *warf* es die Treppe *hinunter.*
[One *threw* it the stairs *down-way.*]
They threw it downstairs.

Man *warf* es die Treppe *herauf.*
[One *threw* it the stairs *up-here.*]
They threw it upstairs.

Inseparable Verbs

The other group of compound verbs that you must study is called the inseparable verbs.   Unlike separable verbs, they do not split into components, but remain units under *all* circumstances.   In this respect they are like simple verbs.

Inseparable verbs take the same endings and make the same alterations in their stems (if they are strong verbs) to form persons and tenses as their parent verbs do.   In only one respect do they differ from simple verbs: they do not place a *ge-* before their past participle.

AN INSEPARABLE WEAK VERB

besuchen	to visit (from suchen, to seek)
ich besuche	I visit (present)
er besuchte	he visited (simple past)
wir haben besucht	we have visited, we visited (conversational past)

AN INSEPARABLE STRONG VERB

erfinden	to invent (from finden, to find)
ich erfinde	I invent
er erfand	he invented (simple past)
wir haben erfunden	we invented (conversational past)

How to Tell Whether a Compound Verb is Separable or Inseparable

All compound verbs that begin with *be-, ent-, ge-, ver-, zer-, miss-,* or *er-* are inseparable.   They do not divide into components.

Examples:

besuchen	to visit	(from suchen, to seek)
entstehen	to come into existence	(from stehen, to stand)
erzählen	to narrate, tell	(from zählen, to count)
gehören	to belong	(from hören, to hear)
verstehen	to understand	(from stehen, to stand)
zerbrechen	to shatter	(from brechen, to break)
missdeuten	to misinterpret	(from deuten, to explain)

Note: Do not confuse the *ge-* which is used to form the past participle in simple and separable verbs with the *ge-* which is a part of an inseparable verb.   Consult your dictionary if you are in doubt.

There is no simple rule for identifying separable verbs.   It will help you, though, if you remember the table of separable prefixes given on pp. 75–76 and repeated here for emphasis.   You have already met these words as either prepositions or adverbs.

ab	off	an	at	auf	up	aus	out
bei	by	ein	in	empor	up	fort	away
heim	home	her	hither	hin	thither	los	loose
mit	with	nach	after	nieder	down	vor	before
weg	away	zu	to	zurück	back		

There are some other prefixes, however, which do not lend themselves to easy classification.   Sometimes they form separable verbs, sometimes inseparable verbs, depending upon the meaning of the compound.   You will either have to remember individual verbs, or get into the habit of checking your dictionary.

Forms You Should Remember for German Verbs

As you may have noticed in your study of German verbs up to this point, verb endings are usually very regular. In most cases, if you know one form for a tense, you can work out the other forms in that tense without too much difficulty.

Verb stems, on the other hand, are much more difficult and much more complex, just as in English. If you memorize four basic forms, however, you can make any other form that you need.

1. The Infinitive. From this very useful form you can make (a) all future forms; (b) all *can, may, must* forms; (c) *should* and *would* forms; (d) most forms of the present tense—(you cannot be sure about the he-she-it form); (e) the present participle; (f) the polite imperative; (g) in verbs that you happen to know are weak, the simple past, and the past participle.

2. Third Person Singular of the Present. Memorize this form, since some verbs alter their stem vowel to make it. It will help you to form (a) the *du* forms (see p. 61); (b) the familiar singular imperative.

3. Simple Past Tense. In strong verbs this is irregular, hence should be memorized.

4. The Past Participle, plus auxiliary it takes. The past participle will indicate (a) whether the verb is simple, separable, or inseparable. It will enable you to form (b) the present perfect, also called the conversational past; (c) the past perfect; (d) all the passive forms.

INFIN.	3RD SING. PRESENT	SIMPLE PAST	PAST PARTICIPLE	MEANING
gehen	er geht	ging	ist gegangen	(to go)
sehen	er sieht	sah	hat gesehen	(to see)
kaufen	er kauft	kaufte	hat gekauft	(to buy)
besuchen	er besucht	besuchte	hat besucht	(to visit)
aufhören	er hört auf	hörte auf	hat aufgehört	(to stop)

Telling Time

In German there are at least three different ways to express the time of day, and some are at variance with English usage. For example:

5:15 A.M. can be expressed as:
  (1) Fünf Uhr fünfzehn   [Five hours fifteen.]
  (2) Viertel nach fünf   [Quarter past five.]
  (3) Viertel sechs   [One quarter (on the way to) six.]

You will never be misunderstood and will always be able to express the correct time of day by using the first method indicated, i.e., the hour followed by the minutes.

Note: In Germany the twenty-four hour system for telling time is often used. All railroad and airline schedules designate times by this system. After 12 o'clock (noon) say:

dreizehn (13) Uhr for	1 P.M.
vierzehn (14) Uhr	2 P.M.
fünfzehn (15) Uhr	3 P.M.
sechzehn (16) Uhr	4 P.M.
siebzehn (17) Uhr	5 P.M.
achtzehn (18) Uhr	6 P.M.
neunzehn (19) Uhr	7 P.M.
zwanzig (20) Uhr	8 P.M.
einundzwanzig (21) Uhr	9 P.M.
zweiundzwanzig (22) Uhr	10 P.M.
dreiundzwanzig (23) Uhr	11 P.M.
vierundzwanzig (24) Uhr	12 midnight

Word Order

German Word Order

As you will observe many times before you finish reading or working through this short grammar, German word order often differs greatly from English word order. For this reason we have supplied a literal word-by-word translation of most German sentences, so that you can identify words within sentences, and see how German is structured. This word order may seem very strange, but actually it is very systematic, and can be explained in a few general rules.

We shall discuss word order under three different headings: (1) verbs, (2) direct and indirect objects, and (3) adverbs. As you study these sections, use whatever method of study you find easiest. Some people prefer to memorize the rule, and apply it to each situation; others prefer to memorize a single specific example, and then to set other sentences into the same pattern; others prefer to memorize many phrases and to build up rules on an unconscious basis.

The Position of Verbs in the Sentence

Four general rules can cover the position of almost all the verbs which you are likely to use in German. (As you will learn when you have advanced beyond this grammar, there are further complexities, and for all practical purposes you should be able to express yourself completely with these four rules.) After you have studied these rules, go through several pages of this grammar and examine the German sentences. Try to recognize which rule of verb position is operating, and the reason for it.

Rule 1. This is normal word order, and it corresponds more or less to English normal word order. *It is the word order that is always used unless there is some reason for using another word order.* The subject, with its modifiers, comes first; this is followed immediately by the working verb, its adverbs, objects, and phrases. If there is a non-working verb form (see p. 111 if you are not sure of the difference between a working verb form and a non-working form), it will be placed at the very end of the clause.

Ich habe ein *Rad gemietet.*
[I have a *bicycle rented.*]
I have rented a bicycle.

Sie müssen einen *Umweg machen.*
[You must a *detour make.*]
You have to make a detour.

Herr Schmidt ist ein vorsichtiger Fahrer.
Herr Schmidt is a cautious driver.

Normal word order is used with the following conjunctions: *und* (and), *oder* (or), *aber* (but), and *denn* (for).

Ich habe den Hörer abgehängt *und* ich habe es noch einmal versucht.
[I have the receiver off-hanged, *and* I have it still once more attempted.]
I put the receiver down and tried it again.

Die Reifen sind neu, *aber* die Bremse scheint nicht zuverlässig zu sein.
[The tires are new, *but* the brake seems not dependable to be.]
The tires are new, but the brake does not seem to be dependable.

Rule 2. This is the usual word order for asking a question, and it corresponds very closely to English question word order.

On the whole, if you begin an English sentence with a verb, you can also begin the German sentence with a working verb.

As in English, the subject then follows.   If there are any non-working verb forms, they go to the end of the sentence.

Kann ich hier ein Rad *mieten?*
[*Can I* here a bicycle *rent?*]
Can I rent a bicycle here?

Haben Sie Ihr Gepäck *vorausgeschickt?*
[*Have you* your baggage in *advance sent?*]
Have you sent your baggage on in advance?

Rule 3.   This rule covers inverted word order.   It has no exact parallel in modern English, although in archaic poetic language we occasionally use something like it.   Stated most simply, the rule for inverted word order is that if *anything* begins a sentence or clause other than the subject: the working verb follows whatever comes first; the subject comes after the working verb; the objects and adverbial constructions come after the subject; and the non-working verb forms are placed at the end.   Presented schematically, the word order is

Introductory element	verb	subject	objects adverbial items	non-working verb forms.

As you will see, this is closely related to the question word order of Rule 2.

Gestern *sind wir* auf den Turm des Domes *gestiegen.*
[Yesterday *have we* upon the tower of the cathedral *climbed.*]
Yesterday we climbed the tower of the cathedral.

Im Ratskeller *haben wir* Wein *getrunken.*
[In the Ratskeller *have we* wine *drunk.*]
We drank some wine in the Ratskeller.

Da wir kein Geld mehr haben, können wir kein *Billett kaufen.*
[Because we no money more have, can we no *ticket buy.*]
Because we have no more money, we cannot buy a ticket.

Äpfel essen wir gern, aber nicht Birnen.
[Apples eat we gladly, but not pears.]
We like to eat apples, but not pears.

Wieviel *kostet* dies *Glas* aus Böhmen?
[How much. *costs* this *glass* from Bohemia?]
How much does this Bohemian glass cost?

Was *wünschen Sie,* bitte?
[What *wish you,* please?]
What will you have, sir?

In the first example, an adverb comes first in the sentence, thereby causing the remainder of the sentence to fall into inverted word order. In the second sentence, a phrase serves as a beginning; in the third sentence, an entire clause, *Da wir kein Geld mehr haben,* causes the second clause to invert its word order. In the fourth sentence the object begins the sentence instead of the subject. The last two examples, it should be observed, begin with various question words and expressions. In such examples, the word order approximates English.

Rule 4. This rule has no parallel in English. It is used with clauses that begin with a relative pronoun (see p. 44) or with one of a group of conjunctions, of which the following are the most common:

als	when	bevor	before
bis	until	da	since
dass	that	seitdem	since
			(in temporal sense)
wenn	if	ob	whether
		obgleich	although
als ob	as if	weil	because
nachdem	after	wie	how

In such clauses, the verbs are all placed at the end of the clause, with the working verb placed at the very end. A list of examples follows:

Er sagt, *dass* kein Zimmer frei *ist.*
[He says, *that* no room free *is.*]
He says that there are no vacant rooms.

Ich weiss nicht, *ob* ich heute *ankomme.*
[I know not, *whether* I today *arrive.*]
I don't know whether I'll arrive today.

Wir kaufen es nicht, *weil* es zu teuer *ist.*
[We buy it not, *because* it too expensive *is.*]
We are not buying it because it is too expensive.

Wissen Sie, *wo* das Postamt *ist*?
[Know you, *where* the post office *is*?]
Do you know where the post office is?

Hier ist das Hotel, *in dem* noch Zimmer frei *sind.*
[Here is the hotel, in *which* still rooms free *are.*]
Here is the hotel in which there are still rooms available.

Wir können nicht kommen, *weil* wir nach Berlin *gehen werden.*
[We can not come, *because* we to Berlin *go shall.*]
We cannot come because we shall go to Berlin.

Die Kirche, *deren* Turm man von hier *sehen kann,* liegt in der Stadtmitte.
[The church, *whose* tower one from here *see can,* lies in the town middle.]
The church, the tower of which is visible from here, stands in the center of town.

These four rules cover almost all aspects of verb position for simple verbs. (For a discussion of the behavior of separable and inseparable verbs, see pp. 76 to 80.) For other specific examples that fit these general rules, read the sections on the future tense (p. 63), the passive (p. 66), the conversational past (p. 56), would and should (p. 70), and can, may, and must (p. 67).

Avoiding Intricate Word Order

It is usually possible to avoid the more complex forms of German word order simply by restating your thought in a simpler form. Instead of translating your thought word for word, phrase for phrase from English, try at first expressing yourself in the simplest sentences possible.

In other words, to avoid difficulties in German, try to use simple constructions.   With a little practice you will be able to avoid quite a few difficult situations without sliding into inaccuracy or baby talk.

The first two types of German word order, described under Rules 1 and 2, should give you no trouble, since they correspond very closely to English word order.   If Rules 3 and 4 seem difficult, you can avoid many difficulties by rephrasing your thought.

INSTEAD OF SAYING:	SAY:
In the Ratskeller we drank some wine.	We drank some wine in the Ratskeller.
Because we have no more money, we cannot buy tickets for the theatre.	We have no more money and we cannot buy tickets for the theatre.
Even though we felt very seasick, we took a walk around the deck.	We felt seasick, but we took a walk around the deck.
The waiter whom we forgot to tip yesterday has just given us a dirty look.	That waiter has just given us a dirty look. We forgot to tip him yesterday.

You can avoid the rather difficult *dass* construction* (Rule 4) in quoting another person's comments, simply by omitting *dass* (that) in your sentence.   In this case your sentence uses ordinary word order.

INSTEAD OF SAYING:	SAY:
He told me that he paid five marks for it.	He told me he paid five marks for it.

* *Dass* (that) may only be omitted in this type of construction, i.e., when you are quoting a statement, thought, or wish.

Word Order of Adverbs and Objects

After you have thoroughly familiarized yourself with the basic rules for verb position which have been presented in the previous sections, you should be ready to learn the following, less important rules.

Direct objects and indirect objects (see p. 116) do not always occupy the same position in the sentence as they do in English. Two basic rules, however, govern the position of these elements.

Rule 1.   If the direct object is a noun, it follows the indirect object.

Ich habe *dem Portier den Zimmerschlüssel* gegeben.
[I have to *the desk clerk the room key* given.]
I have given the room key to the desk clerk.

Ich habe *ihm den Zimmerschlüssel* gegeben.
[I have *to him the room key* given.]
I have given him the room key.

Rule 2.   If the direct object is a pronoun, it goes before the indirect object.

Ich habe *ihn dem Portier* gegeben.
[I have *it* (the room key) *to the desk clerk* given.]
I have given it to the desk clerk.

Ich habe *ihn ihm* gegeben.
[I have *it* (the room key) *to him* given.]
I have given it to him.

Observe that *it* in the above sentences is translated as *ihn*, a masculine accusative form.   You use a masculine accusative form because *der Schlüssel* is a masculine noun, and pronouns which refer to it must also be masculine.

The sequence of adverbs and phrases, too, is different from English, which is much more flexible.   In German the sequence of thought is usually: (1) time (2) manner (3) place.

Wir haben ihn gestern abend glücklicherweise im Hotel angetroffen.

[We have him yesterday evening (time) fortunately (manner) in the hotel (place) met.]

Fortunately, we met him last night in the hotel.

It is always possible, however, to begin a sentence or clause with a phrase or an adverb, as was discussed under verb word order (p. 86).

Glücklicherweise haben wir ihn nicht angetroffen.

[*Fortunately*, have we him not met.]

Fortunately, we did not meet him.

Appendix

Questions of German Spelling and Punctuation

Capital letters: In German capital letters begin (a) the first word of a sentence, as in English; (b) all nouns, as used to be done in Renaissance English, and adjectives used as nouns; (c) all forms of the polite pronoun *Sie*: *Sie, Ihnen, Ihr*; (d) all forms of the familiar pronoun, *du* and *ihr*, when used in a letter. Note that the word for I, *ich*, is not capitalized, unless it happens to be the first word in a sentence. Adjectives of nationality are not capitalized.

Der deutsche Bundeskanzler.
The German chancellor.

Punctuation: In general, German punctuation is the same as in English. There are only two major differences:

(a) dependent clauses are always preceded by a comma and followed by a comma, unless a final mark of punctuation is called for.

Das Buch, das von Dover veröffentlicht wird, kostet zwei Dollar.
[The book, which by Dover published is, costs two dollars.]
The book which is published by Dover costs two dollars.

German does not distinguish restrictive and non-restrictive clauses by punctuation, as in English.

(b) a German infinitive phrase with several modifiers is set off by commas.

Er bat mich, ihm sein Gepäck morgen ins Hotel zu schicken.
[He asked me, him his luggage tomorrow into the hotel to send.]
He asked me to send his luggage to the hotel tomorrow.

Umlaut, a word that has been accepted in English and which you can find in any better edition of *Webster's*, is derived from the verb *umlauten*, literally, *to change sound.* The only sounds that can umlaut are *a* to *ä*, *o* to *ö*, *u* to *ü*, *au* to *äu*. As you note these are all vowels or vowel combinations. The umlaut in German is indicated by the two dots that are placed over the changed vowel sound. In English too, we have the phenomenon of umlaut also referred to as "vowel mutation." When *man* changes to *men* in the plural, or *foot* to *feet*, or *goose* to *geese*, or *mouse* to *mice*, we are actually also in the presence of an umlaut. In former times all the umlauted vowels in German were indicated by an *e* that followed the vowel and you may still encounter this spelling at times. The German poet's name Goethe is a good example. Also cf.: Bürgermeister, Buergermeister, Löwe, Loewe. In fact, the little dots (also called diacritical marks) originated from the *e* which in the Middle Ages was placed above the vowel, this way *ȏ*. Eventually the scribes became tired of writing the complete letter *e* and gradually it was transformed into first two small lines, and then two dots.

The Digraph ß: In many German books the consonant combination *sz* is written as one character (ß); it is equally customary to substitute double *s* (*ss*) for *sz*. This booklet, as well as *Listen and Learn German,* uses double *ss*, but you should also become familiar with the digraph, since you will encounter it in books and newspapers.

An Outline of the German Cases and Their Uses

This section summarizes briefly the four German cases and their uses. It is not intended to be exhaustive, but it will indicate the most important uses to which each case is put. For a discussion of the concept of case itself, see p. 113.

Nominative Case:

(a) The subject of a clause or sentence.

Das Lied hat eine schöne Melodie.
The song has a pretty melody.

(b) Predicate nominatives (see p. 112 for a definition) after verbs of being, becoming, appearing, etc.—*sein* (to be), *scheinen* (to seem), *werden* (to become), *bleiben* (to remain), etc.

Er ist der *beste Reiseführer.*
He is the *best guide.*

Er ist und bleibt *mein guter Freund.*
He is and remains *my good friend.*

Er wird *Lehrer.*
He is becoming *a teacher.*

Genitive Case:

(a) Possession, attribution, material—in most of the situations corresponding to the English possessive in -'s or the English "of-construction."

Das ist der Pass *meines Sohnes.*
[This is the passport *of my son.*]
This is my son's passport.

(b) With certain prepositions which always take the genitive:

während	during	statt (or anstatt)	instead of
wegen	on account of	trotz	despite, in spite of
innerhalb	inside of	ausserhalb	outside of
jenseits	that side of	diesseits	this side of

Während des Regens waren wir im Kino.
[*During* the rain were we in the movies.]
During the rain we were at the movies.

Statt des erwarteten Regens hat die Sonne geschienen.
[*Instead of* the expected rain, has the sun shone.]
Instead of the expected rain, the sun shone.

Wegen des Regens sind wir zu Hause geblieben.
[*On account of* the rain are we at home stayed.]
On account of the rain we stayed at home.

Dative Case:

(a) Indirect objects, as in English.

Er gibt *dem Reiseführer* ein Trinkgeld.
He gives *the guide* a tip.

(b) With certain prepositions which always take the dative:

aus	out of	seit	since
bei	by	von	from, of
mit	with	zu	to
nach	after		

Sie kommt *aus dem Haus.*
She comes *out of the house.*

Er ist der Vater *von fünf Kindern.*
He is the father *of five children.*

(Most instances of the genitive given above in section Genitive Case, (a) may also be expressed by *von* with the dative, though the former is preferred.)   Example: Das ist der Pass *von meinem Sohn.*

(c) With certain prepositions which take the dative in some situations and some meanings:

an	at, on, to	neben	beside, next to
auf	on, upon	über	over, above, across, about
hinter	behind	unter	under, beneath, among
in	in	vor	before, in front of, ago

These prepositions take the dative when no change of position is involved. An easy rule of thumb consists of asking the question *where?* or *when?* (In other situations, involving change of position, or motion towards, these prepositions take the accusative.)

Er reitet *auf einem Pferd.*
He is riding *on a horse.* (Dative, no change of position is involved.)

Wir stehen *vor dem Rathaus.*
We stand *before the city hall.* (Dative)

(d) With certain verbs that take their objects in the dative:

danken	to thank	gehören	to belong to
folgen	to follow	helfen	to help

Der Koffer gehört *meinem Freund.*
The suitcase belongs *to my friend.*

Accusative Case:

(a) Direct objects.
Wir schreiben *einen Brief.*
We write *a letter.*

(b) With certain prepositions which always take the accusative

bis	to, until, as far as	für	for
ohne	without	wider	against, contrary
durch	through	gegen	against
um	around		

Wir fahren *durch die Stadt.*
We travel *through the city.*

Sie fährt *um den Platz.*
She drives *around the square.*

(c) With certain prepositions which sometimes take the dative and sometimes the accusative:

an*	at, on, to	neben	beside, next to
auf*	on, upon, on to	über*	over, above, across, about
hinter	behind	unter	under, beneath, among
in	in, into	vor	before, in front of, ago

These prepositions take the accusative when a change of position is involved. As easy rule of thumb is to ask *where to?* They all involve motion towards something.

Wir gehen *vor das Rathaus.*
We are going *in front of the city hall.*

Wir setzten uns *auf die Bank.*
We sat down *upon the bench.*

---

* For an additional rule concerning *an*, *auf*, and *über*, see p. 48 .

Ich gehe *in die Stadt* spazieren.
I am walking *into the city.*

If the last sentence were to use the dative, *Ich gehe in der Stadt spazieren*, the meaning would be necessarily different. It would mean "I am walking about in the city."

List of Common Strong and Irregular Verbs

Do not memorize this table but read it through a number of times with full awareness of the changes of each verb and the pattern it follows.   It is best to master the parts of each verb as given below when you first learn the verb.   (Only one meaning is given for most verbs.   Consult a dictionary for further meanings.)

ENGLISH MEANING	PRES. INF.	PAST IND. (Simple past)	PAST PART.	3RD PER. SING. PRES.
bake	backen	buk *or* backte	hat gebacken	bäckt
command	befehlen	befahl	hat befohlen	befiehlt
begin	beginnen	begann	hat begonnen	beginnt
bite	beissen	biss	hat gebissen	beisst
prove	beweisen	bewies	hat bewiesen	beweist
bend	biegen	bog	hat gebogen	biegt
offer	bieten	bot	hat geboten	bietet
bind	binden	band	hat gebunden	bindet
ask, beg	bitten	bat	hat gebeten	bittet
blow	blasen	blies	hat geblasen	bläst
remain	bleiben	blieb	ist geblieben	bleibt
roast	braten	briet	hat gebraten	brät
break	brechen	brach	hat gebrochen	bricht
receive	empfangen	empfing	hat empfangen	empfängt
recommend	empfehlen	empfahl	hat empfohlen	empfiehlt
feel	empfinden	empfand	hat empfunden	empfindet

ENGLISH MEANING	PRES. INF.	PAST IND. (Simple past)	PAST PART.	3RD PER. SING. PRES.
appear	erscheinen	erschien	ist erschienen	erscheint
be alarmed	erschrecken	erschrak	ist erschrocken	erschrickt
eat	essen	ass	hat gegessen	isst
drive, go	fahren	fuhr	ist gefahren	fährt
fall	fallen	fiel	ist gefallen	fällt
catch	fangen	fing	hat gefangen	fängt
find	finden	fand	hat gefunden	findet
fly	fliegen	flog	ist geflogen	fliegt
flee	fliehen	floh	ist geflohen	flieht
flow	fliessen	floss	ist geflossen	fliesst
freeze, be cold	frieren	fror	hat gefroren	friert
give	geben	gab	hat gegeben	gibt
go	gehen	ging	ist gegangen	geht
succeed	gelingen	gelang	ist gelungen	gelingt
enjoy	geniessen	genoss	hat genossen	geniesst
turn out	geraten	geriet	ist geraten	gerät
happen	geschehen	geschah	ist geschehen	geschieht
win	gewinnen	gewann	hat gewonnen	gewinnt
pour	giessen	goss	hat gegossen	giesst
be like, equal	gleichen	glich	hat geglichen	gleicht
dig	graben	grub	hat gegraben	gräbt
grasp	greifen	griff	hat gegriffen	greift
hold	halten	hielt	hat gehalten	hält
hang	hängen	hing	hat gehangen	hängt
lift	heben	hob	hat gehoben	hebt
be called	heissen	hiess	hat geheissen	heisst
help	helfen	half	hat geholfen	hilft
sound	klingen	klang	hat geklungen	klingt
come	kommen	kam	ist gekommen	kommt
load	laden	lud	hat geladen	lädt
let	lassen	liess	hat gelassen	lässt

ENGLISH MEANING	PRES. INF.	PAST IND. (Simple past)	PAST PART.	3RD PER. SING. PRES.
run	laufen	lief	ist gelaufen	läuft
suffer	leiden	litt	hat gelitten	leidet
lend	leihen	lieh	hat geliehen	leiht
read	lesen	las	hat gelesen	liest
lie	liegen	lag	hat gelegen	liegt
tell a lie	lügen	log	hat gelogen	lügt
measure	messen	mass	hat gemessen	misst
take	nehmen	nahm	hat genommen	nimmt
whistle	pfeifen	pfiff	hat gepfiffen	pfeift
praise	preisen	pries	hat gepriesen	preist
advise, guess	raten	riet	hat geraten	rät
rub	reiben	rieb	hat gerieben	reibt
tear	reissen	riss	hat gerissen	reisst
ride	reiten	ritt	ist geritten	reitet
smell	riechen	roch	hat gerochen	riecht
call	rufen	rief	hat gerufen	ruft
create	schaffen	schuf	hat geschaffen	schafft
separate	scheiden	schied	hat geschieden	scheidet
seem	scheinen	schien	hat geschienen	scheint
scold	schelten	schalt	hat gescholten	schilt
shove	schieben	schob	hat geschoben	schiebt
shoot	schiessen	schoss	hat geschossen	schiesst
sleep	schlafen	schlief	hat geschlafen	schläft
strike	schlagen	schlug	hat geschlagen	schlägt
shut	schliessen	schloss	hat geschlossen	schliesst
cut	schneiden	schnitt	hat geschnitten	schneidet
write	schreiben	schrieb	hat geschrieben	schreibt
cry	schreien	schrie	hat geschrie(e)n	schreit
stride	schreiten	schritt	ist geschritten	schreitet
be silent	schweigen	schwieg	hat geschwiegen	schweigt
swim, float	schwimmen	schwamm	ist geschwommen	schwimmt

ENGLISH MEANING	PRES. INF.	PAST IND. (Simple past)	PAST PART.	3RD PER. SING. PRES.
swing	schwingen	schwang	hat geschwungen	schwingt
swear	schwören	schwur	hat geschworen	schwört
see, look	sehen	sah	hat gesehen	sieht
be	sein	war	ist gewesen	ist
sing	singen	sang	hat gesungen	singt
sit	sitzen	sass	hat gesessen	sitzt
speak	sprechen	sprach	hat gesprochen	spricht
spring	springen	sprang	ist gesprungen	springt
stand	stehen	stand	hat gestanden	steht
steal	stehlen	stahl	hat gestohlen	stiehlt
rise	steigen	stieg	ist gestiegen	steigt
die	sterben	starb	ist gestorben	stirbt
push	stossen	stiess	hat gestossen	stösst
rub, stroke	streichen	strich	hat gestrichen	streicht
quarrel	streiten	stritt	hat gestritten	streitet
carry, wear	tragen	trug	hat getragen	trägt
meet	treffen	traf	hat getroffen	trifft
drive	treiben	trieb	hat getrieben	treibt
step	treten	trat	ist getreten	tritt
drink	trinken	trank	hat getrunken	trinkt
do	tun	tat	hat getan	tut
spoil	verderben	verdarb	hat verdorben	verdirbt
forget	vergessen	vergass	hat vergessen	vergisst
lose	verlieren	verlor	hat verloren	verliert
forgive	verzeihen	verzieh	hat verziehen	verzeiht
grow	wachsen	wuchs	ist gewachsen	wächst
wash	waschen	wusch	hat gewaschen	wäscht
become	werden	wurde or ward	ist geworden	wird
throw	werfen	warf	hat geworfen	wirft
weigh	wiegen	wog	hat gewogen	wiegt
draw	ziehen	zog	hat gezogen	zieht
force	zwingen	zwang	hat gezwungen	zwingt

Some Common Verbs with Separable Prefixes †

*ab*lehnen	decline
*ab*ziehen	march (or pull) off
sich in *acht*nehmen	be careful
*acht*geben	pay attention
*an*fangen	begin
*an*halten	stop
*an*kommen	arrive
*an*nehmen	accept
*an*sehen	view
sich *an*strengen	exert oneself
sich *an*ziehen	dress
*auf*führen	perform
*auf*halten	delay
*auf*heben	lift, preserve
*auf*hören	stop
*auf*passen	watch out
*auf*machen	open
*auf*stehen	get up
*aus*führen	carry out
*aus*sehen	look, appear
*aus*sprechen	pronounce
sich *aus*ziehen	undress
*bei*tragen	contribute
*dar*stellen	represent
*durch*führen	carry out
sich *ein*bilden	imagine
* *ein*laden	invite
*ein*schlafen	fall asleep
*ein*schliessen	include
*ein*treten	enter
*fest*setzen	fix, establish
**fort*fahren	drive away, continue
*fort*setzen	continue

† Note that a verb with a separable prefix has the same principal parts as the stem verb. For example *zu-geben* forms its parts like *geben*: *zugeben, gab zu, hat zugegeben, gibt zu* (see pp. 75–76).

*herankommen	approach, come near
*heraufkommen	come up
*herauskommen	come out
*herbeibringen	bring to the spot
*hereintragen	bring in
herstellen	manufacture
*herumlaufen	run around
*hervortreten	step forth
*hinabfahren	drive down
*hinaufsteigen	climb up
*hineingehen	come in
*hinausgehen	leave, go out
hinstellen	put down, place
*hinübergehen	go over
*hinuntergehen	go down
*mitgehen	go along
mitmachen	participate
mitteilen	communicate
nachdenken	reflect
nachgeben	give in
sich *niederlegen	lie down
*teilnehmen	participate, take part
übereinstimmen	agree
umfallen	fall down
umkehren	turn back
vorschlagen	propose
vorstellen	introduce
vorziehen	prefer
*weggehen	go away
weitergehen	walk on
zugeben	admit
zumachen	close
*zurückkehren	turn back, return
zurückkommen	come back
*zusammensetzen	put together
zusehen	watch, look on

Note: Many other separable verbs can be made up with the aid of the prefixes used in the above examples. For example, *zurückgeben*, formed with the prefix *zurück* and the verb *geben*, means *to give back*.

The prefixes which are indicated in the above list by an asterisk always have the same meaning, and you can feel free to use them to make up verb compounds of your own. However, the meanings of the other prefixes change and you should consult the vocabulary in *Listen and Learn German* or a dictionary instead of coining new word compounds using these prefixes.

A Glossary of Grammatical Terms

E. F. Bleiler

This section is intended to refresh your memory of grammatical terms or to clear up difficulties you may have had in understanding them. Before you work through the grammar, you should have a reasonably clear idea what the parts of speech and parts of a sentence are. This is not for reasons of pedantry, but simply because it is easier to talk about grammar if we agree upon terms. Grammatical terminology is as necessary to the study of grammar as the names of automobile parts are to garagemen.

This list is not exhaustive, and the definitions do not pretend to be complete, or to settle points of interpretation that grammarians have been disputing for the past several hundred years. It is a working analysis rather than a scholarly investigation. The definitions given, however, represent most typical American usage, and should serve for basic use.

The Parts of Speech

English words can be divided into eight important groups: nouns, adjectives, articles, verbs, adverbs, pronouns, prepositions, and conjunctions. The boundaries between one group of words and another are sometimes vague and ill-felt in English, but a good dictionary, like the Webster Collegiate, can help you make decisions in questionable cases. Always bear in mind, however, that the way a word is used in a sentence may be just as important as the nature of the word itself in deciding what part of speech the word is.

Nouns. *Nouns* are the *words* for *things* of all *sorts*, whether these *things* are real *objects* that you can see, or *ideas*, or *places*, or *qualities*, or *groups*, or more abstract *things*. *Examples* of *words* that are *nouns* are *cat, vase, door, shrub, wheat, university, mercy, intelligence, ocean, plumber, pleasure, society, army.*   If you are in *doubt* whether a given *word* is a *noun,* try putting the *word* "my," or "this," or "large" (or some other *adjective*) in *front* of it.   If it makes *sense* in the *sentence* the *chances* are that the *word* in *question* is a *noun.*   [All the *words* in *italics* in this *paragraph* are *nouns.*]

Adjectives.   Adjectives are the words which delimit or give you *specific* information about the *various* nouns in a sentence.   They tell you size, color, weight, pleasantness, and many *other* qualities. *Such* words as *big, expensive, terrible, insipid, hot, delightful, ruddy, informative* are all *clear* adjectives.   If you are in *any* doubt whether a *certain* word is an adjective, add -er to it, or put the word "more" or "too" in front of it.   If it makes *good* sense in the sentence, and does not end in -ly, the chances are that it is an adjective.   (Pronoun-adjectives will be described under pronouns.)   [The adjectives in the *above* sentences are in italics.]

Articles.   There are only two kinds of articles in English, and they are easy to remember.   The definite article is "the" and the indefinite article is "a" or "an."

Verbs.   Verbs *are* the words that *tell* what action, or condition, or relationship *is going* on.   Such words as *was, is, jumps, achieved, keeps, buys, sells, has finished, run, will have, may, should pay, indicates are* all verb forms.   *Observe* that a verb *can be composed* of more than one word, as *will have* and *should pay,* above; these *are called* compound verbs.   As a rough guide for verbs, *try adding* -ed to the word you *are wondering* about, or *taking* off an -ed that *is* already there.   If it *makes* sense, the chances *are* that it *is* a verb.   (This *does* not always *work,* since the so-called strong or irregular verbs *make* forms by *changing* their middle vowels, like *spring, sprang, sprung.*)   [Verbs in this paragraph *are* in italics.]

Adverbs.   An adverb is a word that supplies additional information about a verb, an adjective, or another adverb.   It *usually* indicates time, or manner, or place, or degree.   It tells you *how,* or *when,* or *where,* or to what degree things are happening.

Such words as *now, then, there, not, anywhere, never, somehow, always, very,* and most words ending in -ly are *ordinarily* adverbs. [Italicized words are adverbs.]

Pronouns. Pronouns are related to nouns, and take their place. (Some grammars and dictionaries group pronouns and nouns together as substantives.) *They* mention persons, or objects of any sort without actually giving their names.

There are several different kinds of pronouns. (1) Personal pronouns: by a grammatical convention *I, we, me, mine, us, ours* are called first person pronouns, since *they* refer to the speaker; *you* and *yours* are called second person pronouns, since *they* refer to the person addressed; and *he, him, his, she, her, hers, they, them, theirs* are called third person pronouns since *they* refer to the things or persons discussed. (2) Demonstrative pronouns: *this, that, these, those.* (3) Interrogative, or question, pronouns: *who, whom, what, whose, which.* (4) Relative pronouns, or pronouns *which* refer back to something already mentioned: *who, whom, that, which.* (5) Others: *some, any, anyone, no one, other, whichever, none,* etc.

Pronouns are difficult for *us,* since our categories are not as clear as in some other languages, and *we* use the same words for *what* foreign-language speakers see as different situations. First, our interrogative and relative pronouns overlap, and must be separated in translation. The easiest way is to observe whether a question is involved in the sentence. Examples: "*Which* [int.] do *you* like?" "The inn, *which* [rel.] was not far from Cadiz, had a restaurant." "*Who* [int.] is there?" "*I* don't know *who* [int.] was there." "The porter *who* [rel.] took our bags was Number 2132." *This* may seem to be a trivial difference to an English speaker, but in some languages *it* is very important.

Secondly, there is an overlap between pronouns and adjectives. In some cases the word "this," for example, is a pronoun; in other cases *it* is an adjective. *This* also holds true for *his, its, her, any, none, other, some, that, these, those,* and many other words. Note whether the word in question stands alone or is associated with another word. Examples: "*This* [pronoun] is mine." "This [adj.] taxi has no springs." Watch out for the word "that," which can be a pronoun or an adjective or a conjunction. And remember that "my," "your," "our," and "their" are always adjectives. [All pronouns in this section are in italics.]

Prepositions. Prepositions are the little words that introduce phrases that tell *about* condition, time, place, manner, association, degree, and similar topics. Such words as *with, in, beside, under, of, to, about, for*, and *upon* are prepositions. In English prepositions and adverbs overlap, but, as you will see *by* checking *in* your dictionary, there are usually differences *of* meaning *between* the two uses. [Prepositions *in* this paragraph are designated *by* italics.]

Conjunctions. Conjunctions are joining-words. They enable you to link words *or* groups of words into larger units, *and* to build compound *or* complex sentences out of simple sentence units. Such words as *and, but, although, or, unless*, are typical conjunctions. *Although* most conjunctions are easy enough to identify, the word "that" should be watched closely to see *that* it is not a pronoun *or* an adjective. [Conjunctions italicized.]

Words about Verbs

Verbs are responsible for most of the terminology in this short grammar. The basic terms are:

Conjugation. In many languages verbs fall into natural groups, according to the way they make their forms. These groupings are called conjugations, and are an aid to learning grammatical structure. Though it may seem difficult at first to speak of First and Second Conjugations, these are simply short ways of saying that verbs belonging to these classes make their forms according to certain consistent rules, which you can memorize.

Infinitive. This is the basic form which most dictionaries give for verbs in most languages, and in most languages it serves as the basis for classifying verbs. In English (with a very few exceptions) it has no special form. To find the infinitive for any English verb, just fill in this sentence: "I like to......... (walk, run, jump, swim, carry, disappear, etc.)." The infinitive in English is usually preceded by the word "to."

Tense. This is simply a formal way of saying "time." In English we think of time as being broken into three great segments: past, present, and future. Our verbs are assigned forms to indicate this division, and are further subdivided for shades of meaning. We subdivide the present time into the present (I walk) and present progressive (I am walking); the past into the simple past (I walked), progressive past (I was walking), perfect or present perfect (I have walked), past perfect or pluperfect (I had walked); and future into simple future (I shall walk) and future progressive (I shall be walking). These are the most common English tenses.

Present Participles, Progressive Tenses. In English the present participle always ends in *-ing*. It can be used as a noun or an adjective in some situations, but its chief use is in *forming* the so-called progressive tenses. These are made by *putting* appropriate forms of the verb "to be" before a present participle: In "to walk" [an infinitive], for example, the present progressive would be: I am *walking*, you are *walking*, he is *walking*, etc.; past progressive, I was *walking*, you were *walking*, and so on. [Present participles are in italics.]

Past Participles, Perfect Tenses. The past participle in English is not *formed* as regularly as is the present participle. Sometimes it is *constructed* by adding -ed or -d to the present tense, as *walked, jumped, looked, received*; but there are many verbs where it is *formed* less regularly: *seen, been, swum, chosen, brought.* To find it, simply fill out the sentence "I have ...." putting in the verb form that your ear tells you is right for the particular verb. If you speak grammatically, you will have the past participle.

Past participles are sometimes used as adjectives: "Don't cry over *spilt* milk." Their most important use, however, is to form the system of verb tenses that are *called* the perfect tenses: present perfect (or perfect), past perfect (or pluperfect), etc. In English the present perfect tense is *formed* with the present tense of "to have" and the past participle of a verb: I have *walked*, you have *run*, he has *begun*, etc. The past perfect is *formed*, similarly, with the past tense of "to have" and the past participle: I had *walked*, you had *run*, he had *begun*. Most of the languages you are likely to study have similar systems of perfect tenses, though they may not be *formed* in exactly the same way as in English. [Past participles in italics.]

Preterit, Imperfect. Many languages have more than one verb tense for expressing an action that took place in the past. They may use a perfect tense (which we have just covered), or a preterit, or an imperfect. English, although you may never have thought about it, is one of these languages, for we can say "I have spoken to him" [present perfect], or "I spoke to him" [simple past], or "I was speaking to him" [past progressive]. These sentences do not mean exactly the same thing, although the differences are subtle, and are difficult to put into other words.

While usage differs a little from language to language, if a language has both a preterit and an imperfect, in general the preterit corresponds to the English simple past (I ran, I swam, I spoke), and the imperfect corresponds to the English past progressive (I was running, I was swimming, I was speaking). If you are curious to discover the mode of thought behind these different tenses, try looking at the situation in terms of background-action and point-action. One of the most important uses of the imperfect is to provide a background against which a single point-action can take place. For example, "When I was walking down the street [background, continued over a period of time, hence past progressive or imperfect], I stubbed my toe [an instant or point of time, hence a simple past or preterit]."

Auxiliary Verbs. Auxiliary verbs are special words that are used to help other verbs make their forms. In English, for example, we use forms of the verb to have to make our perfect tenses: I have seen, you had come, he has been, etc. We also use shall or will to make our future tenses: I shall pay, you will see, etc. French, German, Spanish, and Italian also make use of auxiliary verbs, but although the general concept is present, the use of auxiliaries differs very much from one language to another, and you must learn the practice for each language.

Reflexive. This term, which sounds more difficult than it really is, simply means that the verb flexes back upon the noun or pronoun that is its subject. In modern English the reflexive pronoun always has *-self* on its end, and we do not use the construction very frequently. In other languages, however, reflexive forms may be used more frequently, and in ways that do not seem very logical to an English speaker. Examples of English reflexive sentences: "He washes himself." "He seated himself at the table."

Passive. In some languages, like Latin, there is a strong feeling that an action or thing that is taking place can be expressed in two different ways. One can say, A does-something-to B, which is "active;" or B is-having-something-done-to-him by A, which is "passive." We do not have a strong feeling for this classification of experience in English, but the following examples should indicate the difference between an active and a passive verb: Active: "John is building a house." Passive: "A house is being built by John." Active: "The steamer carried the cotton to England." Passive: "The cotton was carried by the steamer to England." Bear in mind that the formation of passive verbs and the situations where they can be used vary enormously from language to language. This is one situation where you usually cannot translate English word for word into another language and make sense.

Impersonal Verbs. In English there are some verbs which do not have an ordinary subject, and do not refer to persons. They are always used with the pronoun *it*, which does not refer to any-

thing specifically, but simply serves to fill out the verb forms.
Examples: It is snowing.   It hailed last night.   It seems to me
that you are wrong.   It has been raining.   It won't do.

Other languages, like German, have this same general concept,
but impersonal verbs may differ quite a bit in form and frequency
from one language to another.

Working Verbs.   In some languages, English and German, for
example, all verb forms *can* be classified into two broad groups:
inactive forms and working forms.   The inactive verb forms *are*
the infinitive, the past participle, and the present participle.   All
other forms *are* working forms, whether they *are* solitary verbs or
parts of compound verbs.   All working verbs *share* this characteristic: they *are* modified to show person or time; inactive verbs *are*
not changed.   Examples: We *have* sixteen dollars.   We *left* at
four o'clock.   We *shall* spend two hours there.   The guide *can*
pick us up tomorrow.   You *are* being paged in the lobby.   They
are now crossing the square.   I *have* not decided.   [The first two
examples *are* solitary verbs; the last five *are* working parts of compound verbs.]

In English this idea *is* not too important.   In German, however, it *is* extremely important, since working verbs and inactive
forms often *go* in different places in the sentence.   [Working
verbs *are* placed in italics.]

Words about Nouns

Declensions.   In some languages nouns fall into natural
groups according to the way they make their forms.   These
groupings are called declensions, and making the various forms
for any noun, pronoun, or adjective is called declining it.

Declensions are simply an aid to learning grammatical structure.   Although it may seem difficult to speak of First Declension,
Second, Third, and Fourth, these are simply short ways of saying
that nouns belonging to these classes make their forms according
to certain consistent rules, which you can memorize.   In English

we do not have to worry about declensions, since almost all nouns make their possessive and plural in the same way. In other languages, however, declensions may be much more complex.

Predicate Nominatives, Predicate Complements, Copulas. The verb to be and its forms (am, are, is, was, were, have been, etc.) are sometimes called copulas or copulating verbs, since they couple together elements that are more or less equal. In some languages the words that follow a copula are treated differently than the words that follow other verbs.

In English, an independent adjective (without a noun) that follows a copula is called a predicate adjective or predicate complement, while the nouns or pronouns that follow copulas are called predicate nominatives. In classical English grammar these words are considered (on the model of Latin grammar) to be in the nominative (or subject) case, and therefore we say It is I or It is he. As you can understand, since only a handful of pronouns have a nominative form that is distinguishable from other forms, the English predicate nominative is a minor point.

In some other languages, however, the predicate nominative may be important, if predicate nouns and adjectives have case forms. In German, for example, there are more elaborate rules for predicate complements and predicate nominatives, and there are more copulas than in English.

Agreement.   In some languages, where nouns or adjectives or articles are declined, or have gender endings, it is necessary that the adjective or article be in the same case or gender or number as the noun it goes with (modifies).   This is called agreement.

This may be illustrated from Spanish, where articles and adjectives have to agree with nouns in gender and number.

una casa blanca	one white house	dos casas blancas	two white houses
un libro blanco	one white book	dos libros blancos	two white books

Here *una* is feminine singular and has the ending -*a* because it agrees with the feminine singular noun *casa*; *blanca* has the ending -*a* because it agrees with the feminine singular noun *casa*. *blanco*, on the other hand, and *un*, are masculine singular because *libro* is masculine singular.

Gender. Gender should not be confused with actual sex. In many languages nouns are arbitrarily assigned a gender (masculine or feminine, or masculine or feminine or neuter), and this need not correspond to sex. You simply have to learn the pattern of the language you are studying in order to become familiar with its use of gender.

Case. The idea of case is often very difficult for an English-speaker to grasp, since we do not use case very much. Perhaps the best way to understand how case works is to step behind words themselves, into the ideas which words express. If you look at a sentence like "Mr. Brown is paying the waiter," you can see that three basic ideas are involved: Mr. Brown, the waiter, and the act of payment. The problem that every language has is to show how these ideas are to be related, or how words are to be interlocked to form sentences.

Surprisingly enough, there are only three ways of putting pointers on words to make your meaning clear, so that your listener knows who is doing what to whom. These ways are (1) word order (2) additional words (3) alteration of the word (which for nouns, pronouns, and adjectives is called case).

Word order, or the place of individual words in a sentence, is very important in English. For us, "Mr. Brown is paying the waiter" is entirely different in meaning from "The waiter is paying Mr. Brown." This may seem so obvious that it need not be mentioned, but in some languages, like Latin, you can shift the positions of the words and come out with the same meaning for the sentence, apart from shifts of emphasis.

Adding other elements, to make meanings clear, is also commonly used in English. We have a whole range of words like to, from, with, in, out, of, and so on, which show relationships.

Mr. Jones introduced Mr. Smith to the Captain is unambiguous because of the word to.

Altering the word itself is called case when it is done with nouns or pronouns or adjectives. Most of the time these alterations consist of endings that you place on the word or on its stem. Case endings in nouns thus correspond to the endings that you add to verbs to show time or the speaker. Examples of verb endings: I walk. He walks. We walked.

Case is not as important in English as it is in some languages, but we do use case in a few limited forms. We add an -'s to nouns to form a possessive; we add a similar -s to form the plural for most nouns; and we add (in spelling, though there is no sound change involved) an -' to indicate a possessive plural. In pronouns, sometimes we add endings, as in the words who, whose, and whom. Sometimes we use different forms, as in I, mine, me; he, his, him; we, ours, and us.

When you use case, as you can see, you know much more about individual words than if you do not have case. When you see the word whom you automatically recognize that it cannot be the subject of a sentence, but must be the object of a verb or a preposition. When you see the word ship's, you know that it means belonging to a ship or originating from a ship.

Many languages have a stronger case system than English. German, for example, has more cases than English (four, as compared to three maximum for English), and uses case in more situations than English does. What English expresses with prepositions (additional words) German either expresses with case alone or with prepositions and case.

Nominative, Genitive, Dative, and Accusative. If you assume that endings can be added to nouns or pronouns or adjectives to form cases, it is not too far a logical leap to see that certain forms or endings are always used in the same circumstances. A preposition, for example, may always be followed by the same ending; a direct object may always have a certain ending; or possession may always be indicated by the same ending.

If you classify and tabulate endings and their uses, you will arrive at individual cases.

German happens to have four cases, which are called nominative, genitive, dative, and accusative. These names may seem difficult, but actually they are purely conventional. They are simply a short way of saying that in certain situations certain endings and stem changes are involved. It would be entirely as consistent to speak of the A case, the B case, the C case, or the D case.

Miscellaneous Terms

Comparative, Superlative. These two terms are used with adjectives and adverbs. They indicate the degree of strength within the meaning of the word. Faster, better, earlier, newer, more rapid, more detailed, more suitable are examples of the comparative in adjectives, while more rapidly, more recently, more suitably are comparatives for adverbs. In most cases, as you have seen, the comparative uses -er or "more" for an adjective, and "more" for an adverb. Superlatives are those forms which end in -est or have "most" prefixed before them for adjectives, and "most" prefixed for adverbs: most intelligent, earliest, most rapidly, most suitably.

Idiom. An idiom is an expression that is peculiar to a language, the meaning of which is not the same as the literal meaning of the individual words composing it. Idioms, as a rule, cannot be translated word by word into another language. Examples of English idioms: "*Take it easy.*" Don't *beat around the bush.*" "It *turned out* to be *a Dutch treat.*" "Can you *tell time* in Spanish?"

The Parts of the Sentence

Subject, Predicate. In grammar *every complete sentence* contains two basic parts, the subject and the predicate. *The subject,* if *we* state the terms most simply, is the thing, person, or activity talked about. *It* can be a noun, a pronoun, or something *that* serves as a noun. *A subject* would include, in a typical case, a noun, the articles or adjectives *which* are associated with it, and perhaps phrases. Note that in complex sentences, *each part* may have its own subject. [*The subjects of the sentences above* have been italicized.]

The predicate *talks about the subject.* In a formal sentence the predicate *includes a verb, its adverbs, predicate adjectives, phrases, and objects*—whatever *happens to be present.* A predicate adjective *is an adjective* which *happens to be in the predicate after a form of the verb to be.* Example: "Apples *are red.*" [Predicates *are in italics.*]

In the following simple sentences subjects are in italics, predicates in italics and underlined. "*Green apples* <u>are bad for your digestion.</u>" "When *I* <u>go to Spain</u>, *I* <u>always stop in Cadiz.</u>" "*The man with the handbag* <u>is travelling to Madrid.</u>"

Direct and Indirect Objects. Some verbs (called transitive verbs) take direct and/or indirect objects in their predicates; other verbs (called intransitive verbs) do not take objects of any sort. In English, except for pronouns, objects do not have any special forms, but in languages which have case forms or more pronoun forms than English, objects can be troublesome.

The direct object is the person, thing, quality, or matter that the verb directs *its action* upon. It can be a pronoun, or a noun, perhaps accompanied by an article and/or adjectives. The direct object always directly follows *its verb*, except when there is also an indirect object present, which comes between the verb and the object. Prepositions do not go before direct objects. Examples: "The cook threw *green onions* into the stew." "The border guards will want to see *your passport* tomorrow." "Give *it* to me." "Please give me *a glass of red wine.*" [We have placed *direct objects* in this paragraph in italics.]

The indirect object, as grammars will tell *you*, is the person or thing for or to whom the action is taking place. It can be a pronoun or a noun with or without article and adjectives. In most cases the words "to" or "for" can be inserted before it, if not already there. Examples: "Please tell *me* the time." "I wrote

her a letter from Barcelona." "We sent *Mr. Gonzalez* ten pesos."
"We gave *the most energetic guide* a large tip." [Indirect objects
are in italics.]

Clauses: Independent, Dependent, Relative.   Clauses are the
largest components/*that go to make up sentences.*/   Each clause, in
classical grammar, is a combination of subject and predicate./
If a sentence has one subject and one predicate,/it is a one-clause sentence./
If it has two or more subjects and predicates,/it is a sentence of two or
more clauses./
There are two kinds of clauses: independent (principal) and
dependent (subordinate) clauses./   An independent clause can
stand alone;/it can form a logical, complete sentence./   A dependent clause is a clause/*that cannot stand alone*;/it must have another
clause with it to complete it./
A sentence containing a single clause is called a simple sentence./
A sentence with two or more clauses may be either a complex or a
compound sentence./   A compound sentence contains two or
more independent clauses,/and/these independent clauses are
joined together with and or but./   A complex sentence is a
sentence/*which contains both independent and dependent clauses.*/
A relative clause is a clause/*which begins with a relative pronoun:
who, whom, that, which.*/   It is by definition a dependent clause,/
since it cannot stand by itself.
In English these terms are not very important except for
rhetorical analysis,/*since all clauses are treated very much the same in
grammar and syntax.*   In some foreign languages like German,
however, these concepts are important,/and they must be understood,/*since all clauses are not treated alike.*   [Each clause in this
section has been isolated by slashes./   Dependent clauses have
been placed in italics;/independent clauses have not been marked./]

INDEX

The following abbreviations have been used in this index: *adj.* for adjective, *conj.* for conjugation, *def.* for definition, *prep.* for preposition, *pron.* for pronoun, and *vb.* for verb. German words appear in *italic* and their English equivalents in parentheses.

A CATALOG OF SELECTED

DOVER BOOKS

IN ALL FIELDS OF INTEREST

A CATALOG OF SELECTED DOVER
BOOKS IN ALL FIELDS OF INTEREST

CONCERNING THE SPIRITUAL IN ART, Wassily Kandinsky. Pioneering work by father of abstract art. Thoughts on color theory, nature of art. Analysis of earlier masters. 12 illustrations. 80pp. of text. 5⅜ x 8½.   0-486-23411-8

CELTIC ART: The Methods of Construction, George Bain. Simple geometric techniques for making Celtic interlacements, spirals, Kells-type initials, animals, humans, etc. Over 500 illustrations. 160pp. 9 x 12. (Available in U.S. only.)   0-486-22923-8

AN ATLAS OF ANATOMY FOR ARTISTS, Fritz Schider. Most thorough reference work on art anatomy in the world. Hundreds of illustrations, including selections from works by Vesalius, Leonardo, Goya, Ingres, Michelangelo, others. 593 illustrations. 192pp. 7⅛ x 10¼.   0-486-20241-0

CELTIC HAND STROKE-BY-STROKE (Irish Half-Uncial from "The Book of Kells"): An Arthur Baker Calligraphy Manual, Arthur Baker. Complete guide to creating each letter of the alphabet in distinctive Celtic manner. Covers hand position, strokes, pens, inks, paper, more. Illustrated. 48pp. 8¼ x 11.   0-486-24336-2

EASY ORIGAMI, John Montroll. Charming collection of 32 projects (hat, cup, pelican, piano, swan, many more) specially designed for the novice origami hobbyist. Clearly illustrated easy-to-follow instructions insure that even beginning papercrafters will achieve successful results. 48pp. 8¼ x 11.   0-486-27298-2

BLOOMINGDALE'S ILLUSTRATED 1886 CATALOG: Fashions, Dry Goods and Housewares, Bloomingdale Brothers. Famed merchants' extremely rare catalog depicting about 1,700 products: clothing, housewares, firearms, dry goods, jewelry, more. Invaluable for dating, identifying vintage items. Also, copyright-free graphics for artists, designers. Co-published with Henry Ford Museum & Greenfield Village. 160pp. 8¼ x 11.   0-486-25780-0

THE ART OF WORLDLY WISDOM, Baltasar Gracian. "Think with the few and speak with the many," "Friends are a second existence," and "Be able to forget" are among this 1637 volume's 300 pithy maxims. A perfect source of mental and spiritual refreshment, it can be opened at random and appreciated either in brief or at length. 128pp. 5⅜ x 8½.   0-486-44034-6

JOHNSON'S DICTIONARY: A Modern Selection, Samuel Johnson (E. L. McAdam and George Milne, eds.). This modern version reduces the original 1755 edition's 2,300 pages of definitions and literary examples to a more manageable length, retaining the verbal pleasure and historical curiosity of the original. 480pp. 5³⁄₁₆ x 8¼.   0-486-44089-3

ADVENTURES OF HUCKLEBERRY FINN, Mark Twain, Illustrated by E. W. Kemble. A work of eternal richness and complexity, a source of ongoing critical debate, and a literary landmark, Twain's 1885 masterpiece about a barefoot boy's journey of self-discovery has enthralled readers around the world. This handsome clothbound reproduction of the first edition features all 174 of the original black-and-white illustrations. 368pp. 5⅜ x 8½.   0-486-44322-1

STICKLEY CRAFTSMAN FURNITURE CATALOGS, Gustav Stickley and L. & J. G. Stickley. Beautiful, functional furniture in two authentic catalogs from 1910. 594 illustrations, including 277 photos, show settles, rockers, armchairs, reclining chairs, bookcases, desks, tables. 183pp. 6½ x 9¼. 0-486-23838-5

AMERICAN LOCOMOTIVES IN HISTORIC PHOTOGRAPHS: 1858 to 1949, Ron Ziel (ed.). A rare collection of 126 meticulously detailed official photographs, called "builder portraits," of American locomotives that majestically chronicle the rise of steam locomotive power in America. Introduction. Detailed captions. xi+ 129pp. 9 x 12. 0-486-27393-8

AMERICA'S LIGHTHOUSES: An Illustrated History, Francis Ross Holland, Jr. Delightfully written, profusely illustrated fact-filled survey of over 200 American light-houses since 1716. History, anecdotes, technological advances, more. 240pp. 8 x 10¾. 0-486-25576-X

TOWARDS A NEW ARCHITECTURE, Le Corbusier. Pioneering manifesto by founder of "International School." Technical and aesthetic theories, views of industry, economics, relation of form to function, "mass-production split" and much more. Profusely illustrated. 320pp. 6⅛ x 9¼. (Available in U.S. only.) 0-486-25023-7

HOW THE OTHER HALF LIVES, Jacob Riis. Famous journalistic record, exposing poverty and degradation of New York slums around 1900, by major social reformer. 100 striking and influential photographs. 233pp. 10 x 7⅞. 0-486-22012-5

FRUIT KEY AND TWIG KEY TO TREES AND SHRUBS, William M. Harlow. One of the handiest and most widely used identification aids. Fruit key covers 120 deciduous and evergreen species; twig key 160 deciduous species. Easily used. Over 300 photographs. 126pp. 5⅜ x 8½. 0-486-20511-8

COMMON BIRD SONGS, Dr. Donald J. Borror. Songs of 60 most common U.S. birds: robins, sparrows, cardinals, bluejays, finches, more—arranged in order of increasing complexity. Up to 9 variations of songs of each species. Cassette and manual 0-486-99911-4

ORCHIDS AS HOUSE PLANTS, Rebecca Tyson Northen. Grow cattleyas and many other kinds of orchids—in a window, in a case, or under artificial light. 63 illustrations. 148pp. 5⅜ x 8½. 0-486-23261-1

MONSTER MAZES, Dave Phillips. Masterful mazes at four levels of difficulty. Avoid deadly perils and evil creatures to find magical treasures. Solutions for all 32 exciting illustrated puzzles. 48pp. 8¼ x 11. 0-486-26005-4

MOZART'S DON GIOVANNI (DOVER OPERA LIBRETTO SERIES), Wolfgang Amadeus Mozart. Introduced and translated by Ellen H. Bleiler. Standard Italian libretto, with complete English translation. Convenient and thoroughly portable—an ideal companion for reading along with a recording or the performance itself. Introduction. List of characters. Plot summary. 121pp. 5¼ x 8½. 0-486-24944-1

FRANK LLOYD WRIGHT'S DANA HOUSE, Donald Hoffmann. Pictorial essay of residential masterpiece with over 160 interior and exterior photos, plans, elevations, sketches and studies. 128pp. 9¼ x 10¾. 0-486-29120-0

THE CLARINET AND CLARINET PLAYING, David Pino. Lively, comprehensive work features suggestions about technique, musicianship, and musical interpretation, as well as guidelines for teaching, making your own reeds, and preparing for public performance. Includes an intriguing look at clarinet history. "A godsend," *The Clarinet,* Journal of the International Clarinet Society. Appendixes. 7 illus. 320pp. $5\frac{3}{8}$ x $8\frac{1}{2}$. 0-486-40270-3

HOLLYWOOD GLAMOR PORTRAITS, John Kobal (ed.). 145 photos from 1926-49. Harlow, Gable, Bogart, Bacall; 94 stars in all. Full background on photographers, technical aspects. 160pp. $8\frac{3}{8}$ x $11\frac{1}{4}$. 0-486-23352-9

THE RAVEN AND OTHER FAVORITE POEMS, Edgar Allan Poe. Over 40 of the author's most memorable poems: "The Bells," "Ulalume," "Israfel," "To Helen," "The Conqueror Worm," "Eldorado," "Annabel Lee," many more. Alphabetic lists of titles and first lines. 64pp. $5\frac{3}{16}$ x $8\frac{1}{4}$. 0-486-26685-0

PERSONAL MEMOIRS OF U. S. GRANT, Ulysses Simpson Grant. Intelligent, deeply moving firsthand account of Civil War campaigns, considered by many the finest military memoirs ever written. Includes letters, historic photographs, maps and more. 528pp. $6\frac{1}{8}$ x $9\frac{1}{4}$. 0-486-28587-1

ANCIENT EGYPTIAN MATERIALS AND INDUSTRIES, A. Lucas and J. Harris. Fascinating, comprehensive, thoroughly documented text describes this ancient civilization's vast resources and the processes that incorporated them in daily life, including the use of animal products, building materials, cosmetics, perfumes and incense, fibers, glazed ware, glass and its manufacture, materials used in the mummification process, and much more. 544pp. $6\frac{1}{8}$ x $9\frac{1}{4}$. (Available in U.S. only.) 0-486-40446-3

RUSSIAN STORIES/RUSSKIE RASSKAZY: A Dual-Language Book, edited by Gleb Struve. Twelve tales by such masters as Chekhov, Tolstoy, Dostoevsky, Pushkin, others. Excellent word-for-word English translations on facing pages, plus teaching and study aids, Russian/English vocabulary, biographical/critical introductions, more. 416pp. $5\frac{3}{8}$ x $8\frac{1}{2}$. 0-486-26244-8

PHILADELPHIA THEN AND NOW: 60 Sites Photographed in the Past and Present, Kenneth Finkel and Susan Oyama. Rare photographs of City Hall, Logan Square, Independence Hall, Betsy Ross House, other landmarks juxtaposed with contemporary views. Captures changing face of historic city. Introduction. Captions. 128pp. $8\frac{1}{4}$ x 11. 0-486-25790-8

NORTH AMERICAN INDIAN LIFE: Customs and Traditions of 23 Tribes, Elsie Clews Parsons (ed.). 27 fictionalized essays by noted anthropologists examine religion, customs, government, additional facets of life among the Winnebago, Crow, Zuni, Eskimo, other tribes. 480pp. $6\frac{1}{8}$ x $9\frac{1}{4}$. 0-486-27377-6

TECHNICAL MANUAL AND DICTIONARY OF CLASSICAL BALLET, Gail Grant. Defines, explains, comments on steps, movements, poses and concepts. 15-page pictorial section. Basic book for student, viewer. 127pp. $5\frac{3}{8}$ x $8\frac{1}{2}$. 0-486-21843-0

THE MALE AND FEMALE FIGURE IN MOTION: 60 Classic Photographic Sequences, Eadweard Muybridge. 60 true-action photographs of men and women walking, running, climbing, bending, turning, etc., reproduced from rare 19th-century masterpiece. vi + 121pp. 9 x 12. 0-486-24745-7

ANIMALS: 1,419 Copyright-Free Illustrations of Mammals, Birds, Fish, Insects, etc., Jim Harter (ed.). Clear wood engravings present, in extremely lifelike poses, over 1,000 species of animals. One of the most extensive pictorial sourcebooks of its kind. Captions. Index. 284pp. 9 x 12. 0-486-23766-4

1001 QUESTIONS ANSWERED ABOUT THE SEASHORE, N. J. Berrill and Jacquelyn Berrill. Queries answered about dolphins, sea snails, sponges, starfish, fishes, shore birds, many others. Covers appearance, breeding, growth, feeding, much more. 305pp. 5¼ x 8¼. 0-486-23366-9

ATTRACTING BIRDS TO YOUR YARD, William J. Weber. Easy-to-follow guide offers advice on how to attract the greatest diversity of birds: birdhouses, feeders, water and waterers, much more. 96pp. 5³/₁₆ x 8¼. 0-486-28927-3

MEDICINAL AND OTHER USES OF NORTH AMERICAN PLANTS: A Historical Survey with Special Reference to the Eastern Indian Tribes, Charlotte Erichsen-Brown. Chronological historical citations document 500 years of usage of plants, trees, shrubs native to eastern Canada, northeastern U.S. Also complete identifying information. 343 illustrations. 544pp. 6½ x 9¼. 0-486-25951-X

STORYBOOK MAZES, Dave Phillips. 23 stories and mazes on two-page spreads: Wizard of Oz, Treasure Island, Robin Hood, etc. Solutions. 64pp. 8¼ x 11. 0-486-23628-5

AMERICAN NEGRO SONGS: 230 Folk Songs and Spirituals, Religious and Secular, John W. Work. This authoritative study traces the African influences of songs sung and played by black Americans at work, in church, and as entertainment. The author discusses the lyric significance of such songs as "Swing Low, Sweet Chariot," "John Henry," and others and offers the words and music for 230 songs. Bibliography. Index of Song Titles. 272pp. 6½ x 9¼. 0-486-40271-1

MOVIE-STAR PORTRAITS OF THE FORTIES, John Kobal (ed.). 163 glamor, studio photos of 106 stars of the 1940s: Rita Hayworth, Ava Gardner, Marlon Brando, Clark Gable, many more. 176pp. 8⅜ x 11¼. 0-486-23546-7

YEKL and THE IMPORTED BRIDEGROOM AND OTHER STORIES OF YIDDISH NEW YORK, Abraham Cahan. Film Hester Street based on *Yekl* (1896). Novel, other stories among first about Jewish immigrants on N.Y.'s East Side. 240pp. 5⅜ x 8½. 0-486-22427-9

SELECTED POEMS, Walt Whitman. Generous sampling from *Leaves of Grass.* Twenty-four poems include "I Hear America Singing," "Song of the Open Road," "I Sing the Body Electric," "When Lilacs Last in the Dooryard Bloom'd," "O Captain! My Captain!"–all reprinted from an authoritative edition. Lists of titles and first lines. 128pp. 5³/₁₆ x 8¼. 0-486-26878-0

SONGS OF EXPERIENCE: Facsimile Reproduction with 26 Plates in Full Color, William Blake. 26 full-color plates from a rare 1826 edition. Includes "The Tyger," "London," "Holy Thursday," and other poems. Printed text of poems. 48pp. 5¼ x 7. 0-486-24636-1

THE BEST TALES OF HOFFMANN, E. T. A. Hoffmann. 10 of Hoffmann's most important stories: "Nutcracker and the King of Mice," "The Golden Flowerpot," etc. 458pp. 5⅜ x 8½. 0-486-21793-0

THE BOOK OF TEA, Kakuzo Okakura. Minor classic of the Orient: entertaining, charming explanation, interpretation of traditional Japanese culture in terms of tea ceremony. 94pp. 5⅜ x 8½. 0-486-20070-1

FRENCH STORIES/CONTES FRANÇAIS: A Dual-Language Book, Wallace Fowlie. Ten stories by French masters, Voltaire to Camus: "Micromegas" by Voltaire; "The Atheist's Mass" by Balzac; "Minuet" by de Maupassant; "The Guest" by Camus, six more. Excellent English translations on facing pages. Also French-English vocabulary list, exercises, more. 352pp. 5⅜ x 8½.   0-486-26443-2

CHICAGO AT THE TURN OF THE CENTURY IN PHOTOGRAPHS: 122 Historic Views from the Collections of the Chicago Historical Society, Larry A. Viskochil. Rare large-format prints offer detailed views of City Hall, State Street, the Loop, Hull House, Union Station, many other landmarks, circa 1904-1913. Introduction. Captions. Maps. 144pp. 9⅜ x 12¼.   0-486-24656-6

OLD BROOKLYN IN EARLY PHOTOGRAPHS, 1865-1929, William Lee Younger. Luna Park, Gravesend race track, construction of Grand Army Plaza, moving of Hotel Brighton, etc. 157 previously unpublished photographs. 165pp. 8⅞ x 11¾.   0-486-23587-4

THE MYTHS OF THE NORTH AMERICAN INDIANS, Lewis Spence. Rich anthology of the myths and legends of the Algonquins, Iroquois, Pawnees and Sioux, prefaced by an extensive historical and ethnological commentary. 36 illustrations. 480pp. 5⅜ x 8½.   0-486-25967-6

AN ENCYCLOPEDIA OF BATTLES: Accounts of Over 1,560 Battles from 1479 B.C. to the Present, David Eggenberger. Essential details of every major battle in recorded history from the first battle of Megiddo in 1479 B.C. to Grenada in 1984. List of Battle Maps. New Appendix covering the years 1967-1984. Index. 99 illustrations. 544pp. 6½ x 9¼.   0-486-24913-1

SAILING ALONE AROUND THE WORLD, Captain Joshua Slocum. First man to sail around the world, alone, in small boat. One of great feats of seamanship told in delightful manner. 67 illustrations. 294pp. 5⅜ x 8½.   0-486-20326-3

ANARCHISM AND OTHER ESSAYS, Emma Goldman. Powerful, penetrating, prophetic essays on direct action, role of minorities, prison reform, puritan hypocrisy, violence, etc. 271pp. 5⅜ x 8½.   0-486-22484-8

MYTHS OF THE HINDUS AND BUDDHISTS, Ananda K. Coomaraswamy and Sister Nivedita. Great stories of the epics; deeds of Krishna, Shiva, taken from puranas, Vedas, folk tales; etc. 32 illustrations. 400pp. 5⅜ x 8½.   0-486-21759-0

MY BONDAGE AND MY FREEDOM, Frederick Douglass. Born a slave, Douglass became outspoken force in antislavery movement. The best of Douglass' autobiographies. Graphic description of slave life. 464pp. 5⅜ x 8½.   0-486-22457-0

FOLLOWING THE EQUATOR: A Journey Around the World, Mark Twain. Fascinating humorous account of 1897 voyage to Hawaii, Australia, India, New Zealand, etc. Ironic, bemused reports on peoples, customs, climate, flora and fauna, politics, much more. 197 illustrations. 720pp. 5⅜ x 8½.   0-486-26113-1

THE PEOPLE CALLED SHAKERS, Edward D. Andrews. Definitive study of Shakers: origins, beliefs, practices, dances, social organization, furniture and crafts, etc. 33 illustrations. 351pp. 5⅜ x 8½.   0-486-21081-2

THE MYTHS OF GREECE AND ROME, H. A. Guerber. A classic of mythology, generously illustrated, long prized for its simple, graphic, accurate retelling of the principal myths of Greece and Rome, and for its commentary on their origins and significance. With 64 illustrations by Michelangelo, Raphael, Titian, Rubens, Canova, Bernini and others. 480pp. 5⅜ x 8½.   0-486-27584-1

PSYCHOLOGY OF MUSIC, Carl E. Seashore. Classic work discusses music as a medium from psychological viewpoint. Clear treatment of physical acoustics, auditory apparatus, sound perception, development of musical skills, nature of musical feeling, host of other topics. 88 figures. 408pp. 5⅜ x 8½. 0-486-21851-1

LIFE IN ANCIENT EGYPT, Adolf Erman. Fullest, most thorough, detailed older account with much not in more recent books, domestic life, religion, magic, medicine, commerce, much more. Many illustrations reproduce tomb paintings, carvings, hieroglyphs, etc. 597pp. 5⅜ x 8½. 0-486-22632-8

SUNDIALS, Their Theory and Construction, Albert Waugh. Far and away the best, most thorough coverage of ideas, mathematics concerned, types, construction, adjusting anywhere. Simple, nontechnical treatment allows even children to build several of these dials. Over 100 illustrations. 230pp. 5⅜ x 8½. 0-486-22947-5

THEORETICAL HYDRODYNAMICS, L. M. Milne-Thomson. Classic exposition of the mathematical theory of fluid motion, applicable to both hydrodynamics and aerodynamics. Over 600 exercises. 768pp. 6⅛ x 9¼. 0-486-68970-0

OLD-TIME VIGNETTES IN FULL COLOR, Carol Belanger Grafton (ed.). Over 390 charming, often sentimental illustrations, selected from archives of Victorian graphics–pretty women posing, children playing, food, flowers, kittens and puppies, smiling cherubs, birds and butterflies, much more. All copyright-free. 48pp. 9¼ x 12¼. 0-486-27269-9

PERSPECTIVE FOR ARTISTS, Rex Vicat Cole. Depth, perspective of sky and sea, shadows, much more, not usually covered. 391 diagrams, 81 reproductions of drawings and paintings. 279pp. 5⅜ x 8½. 0-486-22487-2

DRAWING THE LIVING FIGURE, Joseph Sheppard. Innovative approach to artistic anatomy focuses on specifics of surface anatomy, rather than muscles and bones. Over 170 drawings of live models in front, back and side views, and in widely varying poses. Accompanying diagrams. 177 illustrations. Introduction. Index. 144pp. 8⅜ x11¼. 0-486-26723-7

GOTHIC AND OLD ENGLISH ALPHABETS: 100 Complete Fonts, Dan X. Solo. Add power, elegance to posters, signs, other graphics with 100 stunning copyright-free alphabets: Blackstone, Dolbey, Germania, 97 more–including many lower-case, numerals, punctuation marks. 104pp. 8⅛ x 11. 0-486-24695-7

THE BOOK OF WOOD CARVING, Charles Marshall Sayers. Finest book for beginners discusses fundamentals and offers 34 designs. "Absolutely first rate . . . well thought out and well executed."–E. J. Tangerman. 118pp. 7¾ x 10⅝. 0-486-23654-4

ILLUSTRATED CATALOG OF CIVIL WAR MILITARY GOODS: Union Army Weapons, Insignia, Uniform Accessories, and Other Equipment, Schuyler, Hartley, and Graham. Rare, profusely illustrated 1846 catalog includes Union Army uniform and dress regulations, arms and ammunition, coats, insignia, flags, swords, rifles, etc. 226 illustrations. 160pp. 9 x 12. 0-486-24939-5

WOMEN'S FASHIONS OF THE EARLY 1900s: An Unabridged Republication of "New York Fashions, 1909," National Cloak & Suit Co. Rare catalog of mail-order fashions documents women's and children's clothing styles shortly after the turn of the century. Captions offer full descriptions, prices. Invaluable resource for fashion, costume historians. Approximately 725 illustrations. 128pp. 8⅜ x 11¼. 0-486-27276-1

HOW TO DO BEADWORK, Mary White. Fundamental book on craft from simple projects to five-bead chains and woven works. 106 illustrations. 142pp. 5⅜ x 8.

0-486-20697-1

THE 1912 AND 1915 GUSTAV STICKLEY FURNITURE CATALOGS, Gustav Stickley. With over 200 detailed illustrations and descriptions, these two catalogs are essential reading and reference materials and identification guides for Stickley furniture. Captions cite materials, dimensions and prices. 112pp. 6½ x 9¼. 0-486-26676-1

EARLY AMERICAN LOCOMOTIVES, John H. White, Jr. Finest locomotive engravings from early 19th century: historical (1804–74), main-line (after 1870), special, foreign, etc. 147 plates. 142pp. 11⅜ x 8¼. 0-486-22772-3

LITTLE BOOK OF EARLY AMERICAN CRAFTS AND TRADES, Peter Stockham (ed.). 1807 children's book explains crafts and trades: baker, hatter, cooper, potter, and many others. 23 copperplate illustrations. 140pp. 4⅝ x 6.

0-486-23336-7

VICTORIAN FASHIONS AND COSTUMES FROM HARPER'S BAZAR, 1867–1898, Stella Blum (ed.). Day costumes, evening wear, sports clothes, shoes, hats, other accessories in over 1,000 detailed engravings. 320pp. 9⅜ x 12¼.

0-486-22990-4

THE LONG ISLAND RAIL ROAD IN EARLY PHOTOGRAPHS, Ron Ziel. Over 220 rare photos, informative text document origin (1844) and development of rail service on Long Island. Vintage views of early trains, locomotives, stations, passengers, crews, much more. Captions. 8⅞ x 11¾. 0-486-26301-0

VOYAGE OF THE LIBERDADE, Joshua Slocum. Great 19th-century mariner's thrilling, first-hand account of the wreck of his ship off South America, the 35-foot boat he built from the wreckage, and its remarkable voyage home. 128pp. 5⅜ x 8½.

0-486-40022-0

TEN BOOKS ON ARCHITECTURE, Vitruvius. The most important book ever written on architecture. Early Roman aesthetics, technology, classical orders, site selection, all other aspects. Morgan translation. 331pp. 5⅜ x 8½. 0-486-20645-9

THE HUMAN FIGURE IN MOTION, Eadweard Muybridge. More than 4,500 stopped-action photos, in action series, showing undraped men, women, children jumping, lying down, throwing, sitting, wrestling, carrying, etc. 390pp. 7⅞ x 10⅝.

0-486-20204-6 Clothbd.

TREES OF THE EASTERN AND CENTRAL UNITED STATES AND CANADA, William M. Harlow. Best one-volume guide to 140 trees. Full descriptions, woodlore, range, etc. Over 600 illustrations. Handy size. 288pp. 4½ x 6⅜. 0-486-20395-6

GROWING AND USING HERBS AND SPICES, Milo Miloradovich. Versatile handbook provides all the information needed for cultivation and use of all the herbs and spices available in North America. 4 illustrations. Index. Glossary. 236pp. 5⅜ x 8½.

0-486-25058-X

BIG BOOK OF MAZES AND LABYRINTHS, Walter Shepherd. 50 mazes and labyrinths in all–classical, solid, ripple, and more–in one great volume. Perfect inexpensive puzzler for clever youngsters. Full solutions. 112pp. 8⅛ x 11. 0-486-22951-3

PIANO TUNING, J. Cree Fischer. Clearest, best book for beginner, amateur. Simple repairs, raising dropped notes, tuning by easy method of flattened fifths. No previous skills needed. 4 illustrations. 201pp. 5⅜ x 8½. 0-486-23267-0

HINTS TO SINGERS, Lillian Nordica. Selecting the right teacher, developing confidence, overcoming stage fright, and many other important skills receive thoughtful discussion in this indispensible guide, written by a world-famous diva of four decades' experience. 96pp. 5⅜ x 8½. 0-486-40094-8

THE COMPLETE NONSENSE OF EDWARD LEAR, Edward Lear. All nonsense limericks, zany alphabets, Owl and Pussycat, songs, nonsense botany, etc., illustrated by Lear. Total of 320pp. 5⅜ x 8½. (Available in U.S. only.) 0-486-20167-8

VICTORIAN PARLOUR POETRY: An Annotated Anthology, Michael R. Turner. 117 gems by Longfellow, Tennyson, Browning, many lesser-known poets. "The Village Blacksmith," "Curfew Must Not Ring Tonight," "Only a Baby Small," dozens more, often difficult to find elsewhere. Index of poets, titles, first lines. xxiii + 325pp. 5⅝ x 8¼. 0-486-27044-0

DUBLINERS, James Joyce. Fifteen stories offer vivid, tightly focused observations of the lives of Dublin's poorer classes. At least one, "The Dead," is considered a masterpiece. Reprinted complete and unabridged from standard edition. 160pp. 5$^{3}/_{16}$ x 8¼. 0-486-26870-5

GREAT WEIRD TALES: 14 Stories by Lovecraft, Blackwood, Machen and Others, S. T. Joshi (ed.). 14 spellbinding tales, including "The Sin Eater," by Fiona McLeod, "The Eye Above the Mantel," by Frank Belknap Long, as well as renowned works by R. H. Barlow, Lord Dunsany, Arthur Machen, W. C. Morrow and eight other masters of the genre. 256pp. 5⅜ x 8½. (Available in U.S. only.) 0-486-40436-6

THE BOOK OF THE SACRED MAGIC OF ABRAMELIN THE MAGE, translated by S. MacGregor Mathers. Medieval manuscript of ceremonial magic. Basic document in Aleister Crowley, Golden Dawn groups. 268pp. 5⅜ x 8½. 0-486-23211-5

THE BATTLES THAT CHANGED HISTORY, Fletcher Pratt. Eminent historian profiles 16 crucial conflicts, ancient to modern, that changed the course of civilization. 352pp. 5⅜ x 8½. 0-486-41129-X

NEW RUSSIAN-ENGLISH AND ENGLISH-RUSSIAN DICTIONARY, M. A. O'Brien. This is a remarkably handy Russian dictionary, containing a surprising amount of information, including over 70,000 entries. 366pp. 4½ x 6⅛. 0-486-20208-9

NEW YORK IN THE FORTIES, Andreas Feininger. 162 brilliant photographs by the well-known photographer, formerly with *Life* magazine. Commuters, shoppers, Times Square at night, much else from city at its peak. Captions by John von Hartz. 181pp. 9¼ x 10¾. 0-486-23585-8

INDIAN SIGN LANGUAGE, William Tomkins. Over 525 signs developed by Sioux and other tribes. Written instructions and diagrams. Also 290 pictographs. 111pp. 6⅛ x 9¼. 0-486-22029-X

ANATOMY: A Complete Guide for Artists, Joseph Sheppard. A master of figure drawing shows artists how to render human anatomy convincingly. Over 460 illustrations. 224pp. 8⅜ x 11¼. 0-486-27279-6

MEDIEVAL CALLIGRAPHY: Its History and Technique, Marc Drogin. Spirited history, comprehensive instruction manual covers 13 styles (ca. 4th century through 15th). Excellent photographs; directions for duplicating medieval techniques with modern tools. 224pp. 8⅜ x 11¼. 0-486-26142-5

DRIED FLOWERS: How to Prepare Them, Sarah Whitlock and Martha Rankin. Complete instructions on how to use silica gel, meal and borax, perlite aggregate, sand and borax, glycerine and water to create attractive permanent flower arrangements. 12 illustrations. 32pp. 5⅜ x 8½. 0-486-21802-3

EASY-TO-MAKE BIRD FEEDERS FOR WOODWORKERS, Scott D. Campbell. Detailed, simple-to-use guide for designing, constructing, caring for and using feeders. Text, illustrations for 12 classic and contemporary designs. 96pp. 5⅜ x 8½. 0-486-25847-5

THE COMPLETE BOOK OF BIRDHOUSE CONSTRUCTION FOR WOOD-WORKERS, Scott D. Campbell. Detailed instructions, illustrations, tables. Also data on bird habitat and instinct patterns. Bibliography. 3 tables. 63 illustrations in 15 figures. 48pp. 5¼ x 8½. 0-486-24407-5

SCOTTISH WONDER TALES FROM MYTH AND LEGEND, Donald A. Mackenzie. 16 lively tales tell of giants rumbling down mountainsides, of a magic wand that turns stone pillars into warriors, of gods and goddesses, evil hags, powerful forces and more. 240pp. 5⅜ x 8½. 0-486-29677-6

THE HISTORY OF UNDERCLOTHES, C. Willett Cunnington and Phyllis Cunnington. Fascinating, well-documented survey covering six centuries of English undergarments, enhanced with over 100 illustrations: 12th-century laced-up bodice, footed long drawers (1795), 19th-century bustles, 19th-century corsets for men, Victorian "bust improvers," much more. 272pp. 5⅜ x 8¼. 0-486-27124-2

ARTS AND CRAFTS FURNITURE: The Complete Brooks Catalog of 1912, Brooks Manufacturing Co. Photos and detailed descriptions of more than 150 now very collectible furniture designs from the Arts and Crafts movement depict davenports, settees, buffets, desks, tables, chairs, bedsteads, dressers and more, all built of solid, quarter-sawed oak. Invaluable for students and enthusiasts of antiques, Americana and the decorative arts. 80pp. 6½ x 9¼. 0-486-27471-3

WILBUR AND ORVILLE: A Biography of the Wright Brothers, Fred Howard. Definitive, crisply written study tells the full story of the brothers' lives and work. A vividly written biography, unparalleled in scope and color, that also captures the spirit of an extraordinary era. 560pp. 6⅛ x 9¼. 0-486-40297-5

THE ARTS OF THE SAILOR: Knotting, Splicing and Ropework, Hervey Garrett Smith. Indispensable shipboard reference covers tools, basic knots and useful hitches; handsewing and canvas work, more. Over 100 illustrations. Delightful reading for sea lovers. 256pp. 5⅜ x 8½. 0-486-26440-8

FRANK LLOYD WRIGHT'S FALLINGWATER: The House and Its History, Second, Revised Edition, Donald Hoffmann. A total revision—both in text and illustrations—of the standard document on Fallingwater, the boldest, most personal architectural statement of Wright's mature years, updated with valuable new material from the recently opened Frank Lloyd Wright Archives. "Fascinating"–*The New York Times*. 116 illustrations. 128pp. 9¼ x 10¾. 0-486-27430-6

PHOTOGRAPHIC SKETCHBOOK OF THE CIVIL WAR, Alexander Gardner. 100 photos taken on field during the Civil War. Famous shots of Manassas Harper's Ferry, Lincoln, Richmond, slave pens, etc. 244pp. 10⅝ x 8¼. 0-486-22731-6

FIVE ACRES AND INDEPENDENCE, Maurice G. Kains. Great back-to-the-land classic explains basics of self-sufficient farming. The one book to get. 95 illustrations. 397pp. 5⅜ x 8½. 0-486-20974-1

A MODERN HERBAL, Margaret Grieve. Much the fullest, most exact, most useful compilation of herbal material. Gigantic alphabetical encyclopedia, from aconite to zedoary, gives botanical information, medical properties, folklore, economic uses, much else. Indispensable to serious reader. 161 illustrations. 888pp. 6½ x 9¼. 2-vol. set. (Available in U.S. only.) Vol. I: 0-486-22798-7 Vol. II: 0-486-22799-5

HIDDEN TREASURE MAZE BOOK, Dave Phillips. Solve 34 challenging mazes accompanied by heroic tales of adventure. Evil dragons, people-eating plants, blood-thirsty giants, many more dangerous adversaries lurk at every twist and turn. 34 mazes, stories, solutions. 48pp. 8¼ x 11. 0-486-24566-7

LETTERS OF W. A. MOZART, Wolfgang A. Mozart. Remarkable letters show bawdy wit, humor, imagination, musical insights, contemporary musical world; includes some letters from Leopold Mozart. 276pp. 5⅜ x 8½. 0-486-22859-2

BASIC PRINCIPLES OF CLASSICAL BALLET, Agrippina Vaganova. Great Russian theoretician, teacher explains methods for teaching classical ballet. 118 illustrations. 175pp. 5⅜ x 8½. 0-486-22036-2

THE JUMPING FROG, Mark Twain. Revenge edition. The original story of The Celebrated Jumping Frog of Calaveras County, a hapless French translation, and Twain's hilarious "retranslation" from the French. 12 illustrations. 66pp. 5⅜ x 8½. 0-486-22686-7

BEST REMEMBERED POEMS, Martin Gardner (ed.). The 126 poems in this superb collection of 19th- and 20th-century British and American verse range from Shelley's "To a Skylark" to the impassioned "Renascence" of Edna St. Vincent Millay and to Edward Lear's whimsical "The Owl and the Pussycat." 224pp. 5⅜ x 8½. 0-486-27165-X

COMPLETE SONNETS, William Shakespeare. Over 150 exquisite poems deal with love, friendship, the tyranny of time, beauty's evanescence, death and other themes in language of remarkable power, precision and beauty. Glossary of archaic terms. 80pp. 5$\frac{3}{16}$ x 8¼. 0-486-26686-9

HISTORIC HOMES OF THE AMERICAN PRESIDENTS, Second, Revised Edition, Irvin Haas. A traveler's guide to American Presidential homes, most open to the public, depicting and describing homes occupied by every American President from George Washington to George Bush. With visiting hours, admission charges, travel routes. 175 photographs. Index. 160pp. 8¼ x 11. 0-486-26751-2

THE WIT AND HUMOR OF OSCAR WILDE, Alvin Redman (ed.). More than 1,000 ripostes, paradoxes, wisecracks: Work is the curse of the drinking classes; I can resist everything except temptation; etc. 258pp. 5⅜ x 8½. 0-486-20602-5

SHAKESPEARE LEXICON AND QUOTATION DICTIONARY, Alexander Schmidt. Full definitions, locations, shades of meaning in every word in plays and poems. More than 50,000 exact quotations. 1,485pp. 6½ x 9¼. 2-vol. set. Vol. 1: 0-486-22726-X Vol. 2: 0-486-22727-8

SELECTED POEMS, Emily Dickinson. Over 100 best-known, best-loved poems by one of America's foremost poets, reprinted from authoritative early editions. No comparable edition at this price. Index of first lines. 64pp. 5$\frac{3}{16}$ x 8¼. 0-486-26466-1

THE INSIDIOUS DR. FU-MANCHU, Sax Rohmer. The first of the popular mystery series introduces a pair of English detectives to their archnemesis, the diabolical Dr. Fu-Manchu. Flavorful atmosphere, fast-paced action, and colorful characters enliven this classic of the genre. 208pp. 5$\frac{3}{16}$ x 8¼. 0-486-29898-1

THE MALLEUS MALEFICARUM OF KRAMER AND SPRENGER, translated by Montague Summers. Full text of most important witchhunter's "bible," used by both Catholics and Protestants. 278pp. 6⅝ x 10.   0-486-22802-9

SPANISH STORIES/CUENTOS ESPAÑOLES: A Dual-Language Book, Angel Flores (ed.). Unique format offers 13 great stories in Spanish by Cervantes, Borges, others. Faithful English translations on facing pages. 352pp. 5⅜ x 8½.

0-486-25399-6

GARDEN CITY, LONG ISLAND, IN EARLY PHOTOGRAPHS, 1869–1919, Mildred H. Smith. Handsome treasury of 118 vintage pictures, accompanied by carefully researched captions, document the Garden City Hotel fire (1899), the Vanderbilt Cup Race (1908), the first airmail flight departing from the Nassau Boulevard Aerodrome (1911), and much more. 96pp. 8⅞ x 11¾.   0-486-40669-5

OLD QUEENS, N.Y., IN EARLY PHOTOGRAPHS, Vincent F. Seyfried and William Asadorian. Over 160 rare photographs of Maspeth, Jamaica, Jackson Heights, and other areas. Vintage views of DeWitt Clinton mansion, 1939 World's Fair and more. Captions. 192pp. 8⅞ x 11.   0-486-26358-4

CAPTURED BY THE INDIANS: 15 Firsthand Accounts, 1750-1870, Frederick Drimmer. Astounding true historical accounts of grisly torture, bloody conflicts, relentless pursuits, miraculous escapes and more, by people who lived to tell the tale. 384pp. 5⅜ x 8½.   0-486-24901-8

THE WORLD'S GREAT SPEECHES (Fourth Enlarged Edition), Lewis Copeland, Lawrence W. Lamm, and Stephen J. McKenna. Nearly 300 speeches provide public speakers with a wealth of updated quotes and inspiration–from Pericles' funeral oration and William Jennings Bryan's "Cross of Gold Speech" to Malcolm X's powerful words on the Black Revolution and Earl of Spenser's tribute to his sister, Diana, Princess of Wales. 944pp. 5⅜ x 8⅜.   0-486-40903-1

THE BOOK OF THE SWORD, Sir Richard F. Burton. Great Victorian scholar/adventurer's eloquent, erudite history of the "queen of weapons"–from prehistory to early Roman Empire. Evolution and development of early swords, variations (sabre, broadsword, cutlass, scimitar, etc.), much more. 336pp. 6⅛ x 9¼.

0-486-25434-8

AUTOBIOGRAPHY: The Story of My Experiments with Truth, Mohandas K. Gandhi. Boyhood, legal studies, purification, the growth of the Satyagraha (nonviolent protest) movement. Critical, inspiring work of the man responsible for the freedom of India. 480pp. 5⅜ x 8½. (Available in U.S. only.)   0-486-24593-4

CELTIC MYTHS AND LEGENDS, T. W. Rolleston. Masterful retelling of Irish and Welsh stories and tales. Cuchulain, King Arthur, Deirdre, the Grail, many more. First paperback edition. 58 full-page illustrations. 512pp. 5⅜ x 8½.   0-486-26507-2

THE PRINCIPLES OF PSYCHOLOGY, William James. Famous long course complete, unabridged. Stream of thought, time perception, memory, experimental methods; great work decades ahead of its time. 94 figures. 1,391pp. 5⅜ x 8½. 2-vol. set.
Vol. I: 0-486-20381-6   Vol. II: 0-486-20382-4

THE WORLD AS WILL AND REPRESENTATION, Arthur Schopenhauer. Definitive English translation of Schopenhauer's life work, correcting more than 1,000 errors, omissions in earlier translations. Translated by E. F. J. Payne. Total of 1,269pp. 5⅜ x 8½. 2-vol. set.   Vol. 1: 0-486-21761-2   Vol. 2: 0-486-21762-0

MAGIC AND MYSTERY IN TIBET, Madame Alexandra David-Neel. Experiences among lamas, magicians, sages, sorcerers, Bonpa wizards. A true psychic discovery. 32 illustrations. 321pp. 5⅜ x 8½. (Available in U.S. only.) 0-486-22682-4

THE EGYPTIAN BOOK OF THE DEAD, E. A. Wallis Budge. Complete reproduction of Ani's papyrus, finest ever found. Full hieroglyphic text, interlinear transliteration, word-for-word translation, smooth translation. 533pp. 6½ x 9¼. 0-486-21866-X

HISTORIC COSTUME IN PICTURES, Braun & Schneider. Over 1,450 costumed figures in clearly detailed engravings–from dawn of civilization to end of 19th century. Captions. Many folk costumes. 256pp. 8⅜ x 11¾. 0-486-23150-X

MATHEMATICS FOR THE NONMATHEMATICIAN, Morris Kline. Detailed, college-level treatment of mathematics in cultural and historical context, with numerous exercises. Recommended Reading Lists. Tables. Numerous figures. 641pp. 5⅜ x 8½. 0-486-24823-2

PROBABILISTIC METHODS IN THE THEORY OF STRUCTURES, Isaac Elishakoff. Well-written introduction covers the elements of the theory of probability from two or more random variables, the reliability of such multivariable structures, the theory of random function, Monte Carlo methods of treating problems incapable of exact solution, and more. Examples. 502pp. 5⅜ x 8½. 0-486-40691-1

THE RIME OF THE ANCIENT MARINER, Gustave Doré, S. T. Coleridge. Doré's finest work; 34 plates capture moods, subtleties of poem. Flawless full-size reproductions printed on facing pages with authoritative text of poem. "Beautiful. Simply beautiful."–*Publisher's Weekly.* 77pp. 9¼ x 12. 0-486-22305-1

SCULPTURE: Principles and Practice, Louis Slobodkin. Step-by-step approach to clay, plaster, metals, stone; classical and modern. 253 drawings, photos. 255pp. 8⅛ x 11. 0-486-22960-2

THE INFLUENCE OF SEA POWER UPON HISTORY, 1660–1783, A. T. Mahan. Influential classic of naval history and tactics still used as text in war colleges. First paperback edition. 4 maps. 24 battle plans. 640pp. 5⅜ x 8½. 0-486-25509-3

THE STORY OF THE TITANIC AS TOLD BY ITS SURVIVORS, Jack Winocour (ed.). What it was really like. Panic, despair, shocking inefficiency, and a little heroism. More thrilling than any fictional account. 26 illustrations. 320pp. 5⅜ x 8½. 0-486-20610-6

ONE TWO THREE . . . INFINITY: Facts and Speculations of Science, George Gamow. Great physicist's fascinating, readable overview of contemporary science: number theory, relativity, fourth dimension, entropy, genes, atomic structure, much more. 128 illustrations. Index. 352pp. 5⅜ x 8½. 0-486-25664-2

DALÍ ON MODERN ART: The Cuckolds of Antiquated Modern Art, Salvador Dalí. Influential painter skewers modern art and its practitioners. Outrageous evaluations of Picasso, Cézanne, Turner, more. 15 renderings of paintings discussed. 44 calligraphic decorations by Dalí. 96pp. 5⅜ x 8½. (Available in U.S. only.) 0-486-29220-7

ANTIQUE PLAYING CARDS: A Pictorial History, Henry René D'Allemagne. Over 900 elaborate, decorative images from rare playing cards (14th–20th centuries): Bacchus, death, dancing dogs, hunting scenes, royal coats of arms, players cheating, much more. 96pp. 9¼ x 12¼. 0-486-29265-7

MAKING FURNITURE MASTERPIECES: 30 Projects with Measured Drawings, Franklin H. Gottshall. Step-by-step instructions, illustrations for constructing handsome, useful pieces, among them a Sheraton desk, Chippendale chair, Spanish desk, Queen Anne table and a William and Mary dressing mirror. 224pp. 8⅛ x 11¼. 0-486-29338-6

NORTH AMERICAN INDIAN DESIGNS FOR ARTISTS AND CRAFTSPEOPLE, Eva Wilson. Over 360 authentic copyright-free designs adapted from Navajo blankets, Hopi pottery, Sioux buffalo hides, more. Geometrics, symbolic figures, plant and animal motifs, etc. 128pp. 8⅜ x 11. (Not for sale in the United Kingdom.) 0-486-25341-4

THE FOSSIL BOOK: A Record of Prehistoric Life, Patricia V. Rich et al. Profusely illustrated definitive guide covers everything from single-celled organisms and dinosaurs to birds and mammals and the interplay between climate and man. Over 1,500 illustrations. 760pp. 7½ x 10⅛. 0-486-29371-8

VICTORIAN ARCHITECTURAL DETAILS: Designs for Over 700 Stairs, Mantels, Doors, Windows, Cornices, Porches, and Other Decorative Elements, A. J. Bicknell & Company. Everything from dormer windows and piazzas to balconies and gable ornaments. Also includes elevations and floor plans for handsome, private residences and commercial structures. 80pp. 9⅜ x 12¼. 0-486-44015-X

WESTERN ISLAMIC ARCHITECTURE: A Concise Introduction, John D. Hoag. Profusely illustrated critical appraisal compares and contrasts Islamic mosques and palaces–from Spain and Egypt to other areas in the Middle East. 139 illustrations. 128pp. 6 x 9. 0-486-43760-4

CHINESE ARCHITECTURE: A Pictorial History, Liang Ssu ch'eng. More than 240 rare photographs and drawings depict temples, pagodas, tombs, bridges, and imperial palaces comprising much of China's architectural heritage. 152 halftones, 94 diagrams. 232pp. 10¾ x 9⅞. 0-486-43999-2

THE RENAISSANCE: Studies in Art and Poetry, Walter Pater. One of the most talked-about books of the 19th century, *The Renaissance* combines scholarship and philosophy in an innovative work of cultural criticism that examines the achievements of Botticelli, Leonardo, Michelangelo, and other artists. "The holy writ of beauty."–Oscar Wilde. 160pp. 5⅜ x 8½. 0-486-44025-7

A TREATISE ON PAINTING, Leonardo da Vinci. The great Renaissance artist's practical advice on drawing and painting techniques covers anatomy, perspective, composition, light and shadow, and color. A classic of art instruction, it features 48 drawings by Nicholas Poussin and Leon Battista Alberti. 192pp. 5⅜ x 8½. 0-486-44155-5

THE MIND OF LEONARDO DA VINCI, Edward McCurdy. More than just a biography, this classic study by a distinguished historian draws upon Leonardo's extensive writings to offer numerous demonstrations of the Renaissance master's achievements, not only in sculpture and painting, but also in music, engineering, and even experimental aviation. 384pp. 5⅜ x 8½. 0-486-44142-3

WASHINGTON IRVING'S RIP VAN WINKLE, Illustrated by Arthur Rackham. Lovely prints that established artist as a leading illustrator of the time and forever etched into the popular imagination a classic of Catskill lore. 51 full-color plates. 80pp. 8⅜ x 11. 0-486-44242-X

HENSCHE ON PAINTING, John W. Robichaux. Basic painting philosophy and methodology of a great teacher, as expounded in his famous classes and workshops on Cape Cod. 7 illustrations in color on covers. 80pp. 5⅜ x 8½. 0-486-43728-0

LIGHT AND SHADE: A Classic Approach to Three-Dimensional Drawing, Mrs. Mary P. Merrifield. Handy reference clearly demonstrates principles of light and shade by revealing effects of common daylight, sunshine, and candle or artificial light on geometrical solids. 13 plates. 64pp. 5⅜ x 8½. 0-486-44143-1

ASTROLOGY AND ASTRONOMY: A Pictorial Archive of Signs and Symbols, Ernst and Johanna Lehner. Treasure trove of stories, lore, and myth, accompanied by more than 300 rare illustrations of planets, the Milky Way, signs of the zodiac, comets, meteors, and other astronomical phenomena. 192pp. 8⅜ x 11. 0-486-43981-X

JEWELRY MAKING: Techniques for Metal, Tim McCreight. Easy-to-follow instructions and carefully executed illustrations describe tools and techniques, use of gems and enamels, wire inlay, casting, and other topics. 72 line illustrations and diagrams. 176pp. 8¼ x 10⅞. 0-486-44043-5

MAKING BIRDHOUSES: Easy and Advanced Projects, Gladstone Califf. Easy-to-follow instructions include diagrams for everything from a one-room house for bluebirds to a forty-two-room structure for purple martins. 56 plates; 4 figures. 80pp. 8¾ x 6⅜. 0-486-44183-0

LITTLE BOOK OF LOG CABINS: How to Build and Furnish Them, William S. Wicks. Handy how-to manual, with instructions and illustrations for building cabins in the Adirondack style, fireplaces, stairways, furniture, beamed ceilings, and more. 102 line drawings. 96pp. 8¾ x 6⅜. 0-486-44259-4

THE SEASONS OF AMERICA PAST, Eric Sloane. From "sugaring time" and strawberry picking to Indian summer and fall harvest, a whole year's activities described in charming prose and enhanced with 79 of the author's own illustrations. 160pp. 8¼ x 11. 0-486-44220-9

THE METROPOLIS OF TOMORROW, Hugh Ferriss. Generous, prophetic vision of the metropolis of the future, as perceived in 1929. Powerful illustrations of towering structures, wide avenues, and rooftop parks–all features in many of today's modern cities. 59 illustrations. 144pp. 8¼ x 11. 0-486-43727-2

THE PATH TO ROME, Hilaire Belloc. This 1902 memoir abounds in lively vignettes from a vanished time, recounting a pilgrimage on foot across the Alps and Apennines in order to "see all Europe which the Christian Faith has saved." 77 of the author's original line drawings complement his sparkling prose. 272pp. 5⅜ x 8½. 0-486-44001-X

THE HISTORY OF RASSELAS: Prince of Abissinia, Samuel Johnson. Distinguished English writer attacks eighteenth-century optimism and man's unrealistic estimates of what life has to offer. 112pp. 5⅜ x 8½. 0-486-44094-X

A VOYAGE TO ARCTURUS, David Lindsay. A brilliant flight of pure fancy, where wild creatures crowd the fantastic landscape and demented torturers dominate victims with their bizarre mental powers. 272pp. 5⅜ x 8½. 0-486-44198-9

Paperbound unless otherwise indicated. Available at your book dealer, online at **www.doverpublications.com**, or by writing to Dept. GI, Dover Publications, Inc., 31 East 2nd Street, Mineola, NY 11501. For current price information or for free catalogs (please indicate field of interest), write to Dover Publications or log on to **www.doverpublications.com** and see every Dover book in print. Dover publishes more than 500 books each year on science, elementary and advanced mathematics, biology, music, art, literary history, social sciences, and other areas.